COMPLEX PTSD RECOVERY:

NAVIGATING THE PATH TO HEALING CHILDHOOD TRAUMA

FAYE MACK

CONTENTS

VOLUME 1

FINDING FAITH

SPECIAL BONUS!

WANT THIS BOOK FOR FREE?

GET **FREE**, UNLIMITED ACCESS TO IT AND ALL OF MY NEW BOOKS BY JOINING THE FAN BASE!

SCAN W/ YOUR CAMERA TO JOIN!

INTRODUCTION

RESCUE

I didn't recognize it at first because it was so tiny. I was walking into our church in the early evening for a meeting, when a movement under a car in the parking lot caught my eye.

It was a kitten. I tried to entice it out from under the car, but it was having none of it. I went on into the church for my meeting.

Some ninety minutes later, the kitten was still there. This time I tried harder to catch it, but it still eluded me.

It was mid-July, and it was hot. The next day I thought to myself, "Surely it can't still be there." Soft-hearted person that I am, I decided to drive by the church and see. Sure enough, it was still there.

Since we have to get on with some serious stuff here, I'll cut this story short. I was to learn that the kitten was a female. She was (and still is) a tortoiseshell (this means she has this lovely, variegated coloring, from black to brown to tan and back again). A half-inch black stripe runs from the tip of her nose back over her head, disappearing behind an ear.

I later learned that she was the lone survivor of her litter. Someone had left a box containing her and her littermates behind the church, I guess hoping that some godly person would take pity on them and perhaps take care of them. I wish *I* were more godly. With the help of some others, I did manage to catch her and take her home.

My spouse and I named her Mira. This was short for "miracle," because we thought it was rather miraculous that she survived the ordeal of her early life.

People who visit us never know we have a cat. After 14 years, Mira runs to her hideout in our bedroom whenever she even *suspects* that anyone else is in the house. We had her spayed, so unfortunately, she could never have children.

She's here now, under my work table, rubbing against my ankle, hoping for a supplement to her breakfast. She has something of a weight problem (I have to be careful that she doesn't see this, as she's sensitive about her weight), so the breakfast supplement is not happening.

Being somewhat clairvoyant, I suspect you're wondering, "Gosh, I wonder what this has to do with C-PTSD and/or PTSD?" Those initials stand for "Complex Post Traumatic Stress Disorder" and "Post Traumatic Stress Disorder."

The answer is that Mira has one of them. She has PTSD, which means that her current condition is the result of one traumatic event in her early childhood, versus a series of such events occurring over time. In a similar way, we as human beings can be traumatized by one incident, such as surviving a serious car accident, or by a series of repeated events occurring over time (such as enduring ongoing sexual abuse as children).

In her weird way, Mira is enjoying a good life. She learns, she adjusts. She has the unfortunate habit of attacking our ankles when we walk by, but we've come to expect and live with this. Mira knows we're the ones who rescued her and provide for her, but some of her alley-kitten habits persist.

Not Your Usual Self-Help Book

I won't be able to take you into my home and care for you; I think we need to be clear about that, given my Mira story.

Some books like this one *do* promise miracle cures, but please don't put this one into that category (this is not the direction I was heading with my Mira story). I'm writing the book because I've been where you are; perhaps I've tried what you've tried to relieve the stress of past trauma.

My own pain led me to do research into the latest and best methods for treating trauma-related stress. I'm confident that what worked for me can work for you. No one is promising that this is easy, but I'm living proof that it is doable!

I will guide you through the research on PTSD/C-PTSD, help you apply what you learn to your specific situation, and see that you come out not much worse for wear on the other side.

So, let's begin by learning more about the differences between PTSD and C-PTSD.

Mira was just here; I won't see her again now till dinner-time.

1

PTSD VS. C-PTSD

A key word in both post-traumatic stress disorder and complex post-traumatic stress disorder is "post." In both disorders trauma has occurred, but the actual occurrence or occurrences that led to them are in the past.

Except, of course, a memory with its attendant feelings lives on in the mind and in the life of the survivor. While a present experience for someone may unfold in a sunlit, forest glade, their being surrounded by bunnies and fawns, the traumatic experience from the past will live again, and turn the idyllic scene into its opposite.

Our minds are blessings, but in certain instances they come to resemble curses more closely, bringing us scenes and thoughts from the past that we would give anything to escape. Some of us turn to drugs and alcohol to escape, but for the most part these simply push the problem deeper, and, in the process, become problems in and of themselves. The term "vicious circle" could have been articulated to describe this situation.

Alcoholism and drug addiction bring temporary numbness, to PTSD symptoms and virtually everything else, and of course logic tells us "Stay away from them!", but as everyone knows who has struggled with substance abuse, drugs and alcohol become powerful "medicines" in the search for calm and peace of mind. As I say, however, the "cure" is often worse than the problem.

SIMILARITIES AND DIFFERENCES

Before delving into the specific disorders PTSD and C-PTSD, I want to talk about our two dimensions of consciousness: These are surface consciousness and subconsciousness. The former we should be able to access with relative ease, as it is basically synonymous with awareness. I know, for example, that my nimble fingers are flying across this keyboard now; that I'm seated at my work table, and that our Christmas tree is still standing in here, even though it's currently the month of March.

In a way, I think of our conscious awareness as similar to the work of an air traffic controller. Impressions from our immediate environment come cascading in, and we need someone "in the tower" to guide them to safe landings. Once on the ground, actual planes have to make their ways to the appropriate gates to dislodge their passengers. In our minds, immediate impressions and their emotional "baggage" also have to be routed to the appropriate storage areas in the subconscious. We can barely imagine how intricate our neural apparatus is in the management and storage of experience, thoughts, and feelings.

If our minds were like pinball machines (I'm from the pinball era versus the digital era), traumatic events are similar to what happens when we ram or push the pinball machine too hard, discombobulating its control mechanisms, and causing it to display TILT. When that happens, the game is essentially over and we have to start again. Everything has to be reset.

FROM THE BEGINNING

A traumatic event is not, as it were, painted on a blank canvas. It is, rather, imprinted on an individual human being who has already accumulated a wealth of experience and a store of emotional and intellectual responses to that experience.

Shall we engage for a moment in the "nature or nurture" debate? Are some people better able to handle trauma than others, either because of their hereditary wiring, or the way they have been raised?

Whichever influencer (heredity or environment) exerts the most impact, that we all vary in our ability to cope with trauma is not in dispute. I have watched a set of twins now from the time they were three days old until the present, when they are nine months old. While they are rather similar in appearance, there are also striking differences in their overall size, the shape of their heads, diet preferences, sleep patterns, play preferences, and overall "affect," the degree to which they let their emotions show.

What is constant in their lives is the way their parents treat them. The twins eat at the same time, nap at the same time, have the same routines for bathing and "tummy time." At around five months of age, because their mother's maternity leave was exhausted, they were obliged to attend day care. I was sure that this was going to be problematic, if not downright *trau*matic, due to the nurturing they'd received to that point.

It was not.

Essentially, they said "See ya!" to their dad early in the morning, went in, had a full day with a batch of their compatriots (I think there are eight of them in their "class"), had snacks, napped, played, and when their mom appeared, said basically (except they can't talk), "Oh hi, Mom!—is it time to go home already?"

This has been the pattern now for the past several months. They come home at the end of the day, get changed, eat, get into their sleepwear, go to bed and sleep for twelve straight hours, then get up and do the whole routine again. Remarkable.

Clearly the twins have developed considerable resilience in the face of change. Now, would this resilience hold up to any kind of serious trauma? I suspect not, in that whatever resistance to trauma any of us develops is years in the making, and even later in life we are never totally resistant to it. What the twins do have is a good start. They are developing a sense that they are valuable, that they can withstand significant change, and that there are constants in their lives they can rely on.

Studies have shown that depriving any new baby, be it human or a rhesus monkey, of love and care in its early days is critical to its mental and emotional development. Should trauma arrive in the life of any of us, we have widely different platforms from which to withstand and overcome it.

EXPLORING THE DIFFERENCES

Kennedy (2020) reviews for us the key differences between PTSD and C-PTSD, starting with the fact that PTSD usually results from one traumatic event, such as an automobile accident, a sexual assault, or the loss of a child. The causes of C-PTSD on the other hand occur repeatedly, such as experiencing sexual abuse as a child, living with domestic violence, or being kidnapped. Kennedy doesn't mention it, but I think about the trauma experienced by captives in the ongoing war between Russia and Ukraine, with Ukrainian prisoners being subjected to weeks and months of torture and rape. By contrast, Kennedy adds that C-PTSD can also occur early in life, is inflicted by someone close to the victim, and is carried out by someone close whom the traumatized individual must continue to see on a regular basis.

PTSD and C-PTSD Diagnoses

We learn from PTSD UK (that stands for Post-Traumatic Stress Disorder U.K.) (2023) that initially there was little to separate the two conditions (PTSD and C-PTSD). The people at PTSD UK remind us that C-PTSD, as of early 2022, was still not recognized as a separate disorder by the "Bible" used for diagnoses by psychiatrists and psychologists, the *Diagnostic and Statistical Manual of Mental Disorders, 5th Edition.*

These experts allege that since there is still debate as to the differences between the two disorders, the best thing for trauma sufferers to do is catalog their physical and emotional symptoms as often as practicable (this means write them down). Doing this allows the professionals to separate the two conditions, diagnose specific symptoms, and arrange the appropriate therapies.

I'm going to cite no one more nor less than Ph.D Dianne Grande (2022) to first list for us the symptoms of PTSD:

- disturbing memories that recur
- bad dreams
- dissociation from the present moment (e.g., "going elsewhere" in your mind)
- flashbacks to the event (visual, auditory, emotional, or physical sensations)
- avoiding people, places, or objects that take you back to the trauma
- being unable to remember
- disturbing ideas about yourself, others, and/or the world, (e.g., "people can't be trusted" or "the world is a terrible place"

- recurring bad moods
- feeling numb to positive emotions
- losing of interest in and enjoyment of things previously enjoyed
- feeling irritable or angry; having angry outbursts
- engaging in self-destructive dangerous behaviors
- being unable to relax (alert for potential threats)
- jumpy, easily startled
- having difficulty concentrating
- experiencing disturbances in sleep patterns (para. 6)

And here is Grande's list of C-PTSD symptoms:

- frequent negative beliefs about yourself
- avoidance of relationships (difficulty trusting others)
- staying in unhealthy relationships
- difficulty managing emotions (angry outbursts or intense sadness)
- high-risk behaviors
- self-harming behaviors
- hopelessness or emptiness
- extreme startle responses
- disturbed sleep patterns and nightmares

- flashbacks
- intrusive, frightening thoughts
- hypervigilance, feeling "on edge"
- irritability
- difficulty in concentration
- loss of interest in previously enjoyed activities
- loss of memory for parts of the traumatic events
- feelings of fear, guilt, or shame
- beliefs that other are "bad" or that the world is generally unsafe (para. 5)

At first, it appears that Grande's lists are very similar (they are), but I encourage you to look again. The word "persistent" occurs only once in the list of symptoms for PTSD; it occurs *three* times in the second list. "Persistent" connotes something that "hangs on," that is difficult to shake.

Note too the list of adjectives in the second list that indicate intensity or *depth* of feeling: "high risk behaviors," "hopelessness or emptiness," "frightening," "angry outbursts," "hypervigilance," and "self-harming." These characterizations shouldn't surprise us, as what differentiates C-PTSD from PTSD is its duration; there is simply more time for more traumatic experience, leading perhaps to a diminishing ability to avoid or forestall it.

Can the Twain Meet?

There are a bunch of TV shows in America about the modification and restoration of automobiles. Among these are *Texas Metal, Iron Resurrection, Fantom Works, Garage Squad,* and *Full Custom Garage.*

The mechanics on one of these shows takes particular umbrage at previous shoddy work done on vehicles. From who knows how far back, the mechanics have taken samples of bad work and welded them into a misshapen sculpture, which they display at the entrance to their property. As additional bad work is stripped from a vehicle, onto the sculpture it goes.

I can identify with the sculpture. I suspect that to a degree we all can. Each of us is an amalgam of connected parts fastened together and stored away in both conscious and subconscious memory. Instead of badly welded ball joints and misapplied fiberglass, we sometimes feature inaccurate and/or disproportionate ideas and feelings about who we are and the potential each of us possesses to be different.

Stephen Covey (*The 7 Habits,* 2004) believes that each of us is created twice. Here is the way he puts this: "...there is a first creation to every part of our lives. We are either the second creation of our own proactive design, or... the second creation of other people's agendas, of circumstances, or of past habits" (p. 100).

Those car shows I talked about? The part I like best is the end of each episode, when the owner of a restored car first sees it. The transformation of vehicles *is* pretty amazing. Not only is there a glistening new paint job, sometimes with new graphics added, but often there is a new engine as well, capable of much-improved performance. Interiors are also redone to exacting standards. Drivers and passengers need to be comfortable in their "new" vehicles.

Do I need to spell out this analogy? Okay. As painful as PTSD and C-PTSD are, there are therapies that both relieve and, in some cases, eradicate them. What seems like a Humpty Dumpty phenomenon really isn't. Pieces can be found, and they can be put back together.

Let's look now at the double-whammy of PTSD and C-PTSD occurring together.

Co-Debilitators

I don't recall why I was as startled as I was when I learned that PTSD and C-PTSD can occur in the same individual at the same time, but of course they can. Think, for example, of the person who returns from war with PTSD from that experience—and also suffered from repeated sexual abuse as a small child. Overlapping distressors.

Davis (2021) enumerates first the symptoms of PTSD:

- spontaneous or involuntary and intrusive distressing memories of the traumatic events
- recurrent distressing dreams
- flashbacks or other dissociative reactions
- intense or prolonged psychological distress at exposure to triggers
- physiological reactions to reminders of the traumatic events
- persistent avoidance of distressing memories, thoughts, or feelings
- inability to remember an important aspect of the traumatic events
- persistent and exaggerated negative beliefs or expectations about oneself
- persistent, distorted blame of self or others
- persistent fear
- chronic guilt
- chronic shame
- lessened interest in significant activities
- feeling detached or estranged from others
- inability to experience positive emotions
- aggressive behavior

- reckless or self-destructive behavior
- hypervigilance
- exaggerated startle response
- problems [of] concentration
- distress or impairment in social, occupational, or other critical areas of functioning (para. 8)

Most of the terms in Davis's list are familiar, but one phrase you may not be familiar with is "dissociative reactions." When someone or something is "with you," that is fairly easy to appreciate and understand. The American Psychiatric Association (2023) helps us understand the reverse of this situation, when we voluntarily or involuntarily "check out of" a given situation.

The APA explains that dissociation can help a person handle what would otherwise be too hard to bear. The individual may dissociate the memory of both a difficult moment itself as well as the memory of the place in which it occurred, plus the circumstances or feelings about the overwhelming event, escaping "the fear, pain, and horror" (para. 6).

Whether from actual individuals or from books, movies, or TV, many of us have heard a person say, "I don't remember anything after that" in reference to a traumatic occurrence such as an automobile accident. Dissociation: excising the event from conscious memory.

Another item on Davis's list is "reckless or self-destructive behavior." I had a friend early in my high school years who had what I thought was a strange relationship with his parents. He was outwardly rude to his mother. He hardly ever said anything to or about his father.

When he was able to drive, he engaged in this terrifying act: In a residential alley, he would get behind the wheel of his car and accelerate down the alley toward a cross street. He wouldn't slow down, let alone stop at the cross street; I know because I was with him on several of these occasions. He would go hurtling down the alley and across the cross street, never braking, often laughing hysterically. Reckless and self-destructive indeed.

Here now is Davis's symptom list for C-PTSD:

- losing memories of trauma or reliving them
- difficulty regulating emotions (they can manifest as rage)
- depression
- suicidal thoughts or actions

- abrupt mood swings
- feeling detached from oneself
- feeling different from other people
- feeling ashamed
- feeling guilty
- having difficulty maintaining relationships
- having difficulty trusting people
- seeking out or becoming a rescuer
- being fearful for no obvious reason
- feeling always on the alert
- becoming obsessed with revenge on the perpetrator
- feeling a loss of spiritual attachment; either ignoring or depending upon religion for self-worth (para. 9)

Seeing this list, I place myself in the position of caregiver, and I want to shout, "No! Don't feel that way! We can fix this!" I'm also ready to trot out my collection of lines from the movie *Zorba the Greek* (1964). In that film, Zorba's young protege Basil makes a comment about trouble, to which the grizzled Zorba replies, "Life *is* trouble! Only *death* is not! To be alive is to undo your belt and *look* for trouble!"

Aren't many of our responses to life predicated on our *expectations*? Is this too simplistic? Don't we tend to tear our hair, lie on the floor, and kick our heels when something doesn't go the way we *think* it should? If only rationality were the cure-all I'd like it to be. If you've known someone subject to panic attacks, you may know what I mean here.

In the latter cases, you can spell out in exhaustive detail that there is nothing to fear. You demand logic from the afflicted party, but logic in these instances is often absent. In fact, it can be a starting place, as we try to "prove" to the other person that nothing in their immediate environment is going to get them.

They know on some level that what's in their *mind* is going to get them, and neither you nor anyone else can convince them otherwise.

What About Religion or Spirituality?

Here again is that last symptom of C-PTSD: "Feeling a loss of spiritual attachment and either ignoring or depending upon religion for self-worth" (Davis, 2021).

The last thing one should do in a book of this type is sound "preachy," and I won't. I *will* tell you about someone in Christian scripture, however, who went from rejecting Christian doctrine and principles to becoming its most dedicated and influential proponent. This was Saul of Tarsus, who became better known as the Apostle Paul. In our book we're talking about the remediation of PTSD and C-PTSD, and Paul certainly achieved this.

While still in his "Saul" iteration, he was among the fiercest persecutors of early Christians. Scholars debate what really happened to Saul on a trip he made to Damascus (Syria) to round up more Christians, but we read that he was knocked flat on that road, struck blind, and was unable to speak. He heard, "Saul, Saul —why are you persecuting me?" He remained in his flat-on-his back-unable-to-speak posture for three days.

The most clear and impactful statement of Paul's conversion appears in his letter to the church in Galatia: "I have been crucified with Christ, and it is no longer I who live but Christ who lives in me. And the life I live now in the body I live by faith in the Son of God, who loved me and gave himself for me" (NIV, Galatians 2:20).

Paul didn't "depend on religion for self-worth." "Religion" refers to a set of beliefs and practices engaged in by a given population and may have little to do with one's peace of mind, actual conduct, or proximity to a higher power. A saying popular in the American South is, "Sittin' in church don't make you a Christian no more than sittin' in a chicken coop makes you a chicken."

What both Jesus and Paul *did* accomplish was something called "death to self." See Paul's words above from Galatians about being "crucified with Christ." Jesus himself said, "For even the Son of Man did not come to be served, but to serve, and give his as a ransom for many" (Mark 10:45).

Our book is devoted to freeing you from PTSD or C-PTSD (or the combination of both). Both Paul and Jesus "stepped out of themselves" in order to accomplish their earthly purposes. To the extent that any of us can do this, the more peaceful and satisfying our lives will be. I hasten to add "the more *inner* peace and satisfaction" we'll have.

Trauma

When we think of psychotherapy, many of us picture a patient lying on a couch, hands perhaps folded across their chest. They are looking up, apparently deep in thought. Nearby is a therapist, legs crossed, taking notes (interestingly, they rarely seem to use laptops or tablets, preferring apparently to jot things down in longhand). The patient, if the stereotype is accurate, is going back in time, relating incidents that bear in some way on their current state of mind.

If I read him correctly, Brenner (2006) suggests that psychotherapy may want to take a more streamlined approach. Brenner cites a book by Colin Ross (2002) called *The Trauma Model* as his primary source. Brenner's conclusion based on Ross's theory, "...offers a cogent explanation for the spectrum of severity of the various mental disorders." Apparently, some patients don't heal as quickly as others. This is caused by mitigating factors of psychic trauma. Ross contends that early psychic trauma is "...the most important contributing factor in all mental illness." To him, "...chronic childhood trauma is to psychiatry what germs are to general medicine" (para. 3).

A key sentence in the foregoing is "the presence of mitigating factors related to the complications of psychic trauma." It is followed by the equally dramatic conclusion that "...early psychic trauma is the most contributing factor in all mental illness."

I will leave it to the wider psychiatric community to debate the merits of Ross's ideas. My reason for including it here is to emphasize the potentially enormous impact of trauma on the pathology of those suffering from PTSD and/or C-PTSD. The condition is real; the road to recovery can be long and winding.

TRIGGERS AND FLASHBACKS

It's little comfort for those suffering with PTSD and/or C-PTSD to hear, "It's all in your mind." To those affected by past trauma, the events that caused the trauma can feel as real in the present as they did when they originally happened.

A triggering event can be anything that takes you back in your mind to actual traumatic experiences from your past. It can be a sensory experience such as a particular odor; it can be seeing a person who resembles someone who assaulted you; it can be being in a room similar to one in which assaults occurred.

My phrase in that last paragraph was "takes you back in your mind'" you "flash back" on the basis of a current stimulus to the traumatic events themselves. A flashback is not the same as a memory or a recollection. A flashback is *reliving* an experience from the past, complete with the feelings evoked by that experience: fear or panic, physical pain, a sense that traumatizing events themselves are happening in the present.

Davis (2022) tells us that "a person who has experienced trauma will experience negative feelings, including intense fear and the need to escape. Further, when memories that flood back are horrific, our bodies will react physically and mentally as though the perpetrator was still hurting us" (para. 8).

The key, according to Davis, is to return in your mind to what is *actually* occurring. She cites the following techniques that facilitate this process:

- Breathe deeply.
- Remind yourself that you are experiencing a flashback.
- Employ all your senses.

"When a disturbing flashback occurs, breathe deeply and then exhale slowly; try to actually feel the air as it expands your lungs. In many cases doing this will help ground you in the present moment and also slow your body's "fight or flight" impulse" (para. 9).

Recognize what is happening! The flashback isn't real, any more than the images projected on a screen by a projector are real. Reading this you may respond, "Duh: Of course I realize it isn't real!" Remember, however, that the flashback can in effect *block out the reality of the present*; you need to re-establish your connection to what's physically happening: who you are now; what's really happening in the present; you are safe from what terrified (traumatized) you long ago (para. 10).

Davis tells us to "look around and list the items in the room, to count the furniture, to breathe in a comforting aroma, and listen to any surrounding noises. Do what you can to engage all five of your senses. All of this should help you return to the present moment" (para. 11).

SYMPTOM CLUSTERS

The following diagram is from the people at Research Gate, prepared by Jovanovich and Norrholm (2010):

Figure 1: PTSD Symptom Clusters

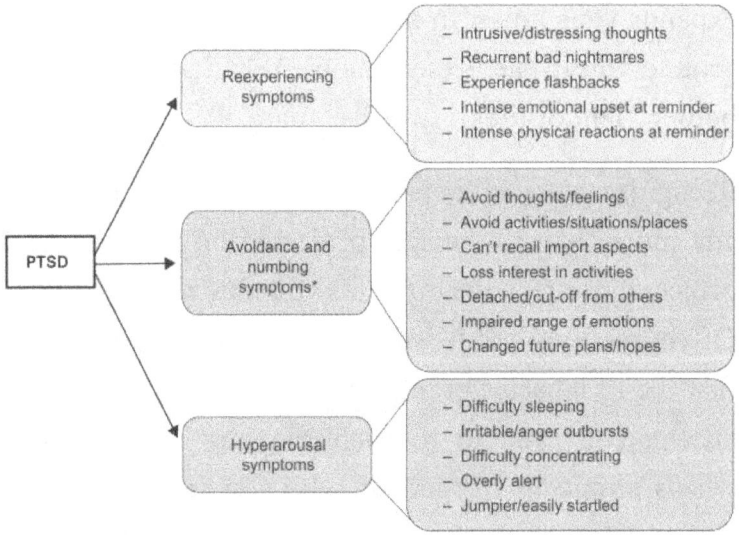

The diagram is not strictly chronological in its depiction of PTSD symptoms, but rather it serves primarily to identify the main components of PTSD (re-experiencing, avoidance/numbing, hyperarousal). What I want you to do is examine the clusters in the third column of the diagram and begin to identify the factors there that may be affecting you.

How these factors operate is the focus of Chapter Two, which begins on the next page.

2

EXAMINING THE IMPACT

WHERE HAVE YOU GONE, ROCK HUDSON?

I'm not going to become a neuroscientist; probably not a neurosurgeon either. I do, however, need to keep the Rock Hudson character in mind from the movie "Magnificent Obsession." In that film, from 1954, Rock plays an irresponsible playboy who is seriously injured in an automobile accident (his fault). Because doctors are involved in *his* surgery, they are unable to save the life of a brilliant doctor, who dies as a result.

Well, this gets even more complicated now. The doctor's widow (Jane Wyman) develops a disease that robs her of her sight. Nothing for it but for Rock to go to medical school, become an ophthalmologic surgeon

(I've learned that this can take up to fourteen years), assume care of Jane, and perform an operation that saves her sight. They fall in love, get married, and probably have a bunch of children.

Only in the movies.

Comparing eye function to *brain* function is like comparing a motor scooter to a Lexus. Let's make it the EV version of a Lexus.

One person's brain is more complex and powerful than the most powerful computer ever created, or that ever will be created. As Choi (2013) tells us, our brain may be an even more robust computer than we imagined, that "microscopic branches" of brain cells once thought to serve mainly as mere wiring may actually behave as minicomputers! Choi estimates that "our brains possess about 100 *billion* neurons with roughly 1 quadrillion—1 million billion—connections known as synapses wiring these cells together" (paras. 1 & 2).

Our co-topics are post traumatic stress disorder (PTSD) and complex post traumatic stress disorder (C-PTSD). Each of these affects brain function in complex ways, and I want you to have at least a nodding acquaintance with how our brains work before getting too far into the nature of PTSD/C-PTSD and their treatment options. Mechanics, after all, read repair manuals before taking wrenches in hand. I know; false analogy. Before you become too proud of yourself... all analogies or comparisons *are* false, in that they are not the phenomena they describe.

THE NEED FOR COORDINATION

On CBS's *60 Minutes*, I recently saw a segment on Volkswagen's enormous Wolfsburg, Germany manufacturing facility. Henry Ford, credited with inventing the automobile assembly line, might not recognize the Wolfsburg facility.

The "production line" in Wolfsburg would indeed be unrecognizable to Mr. Ford. Virtually all mechanical work is carried out by robots. Huge robots. Let me describe the most startling thing to me about this plant. You know, of course, that you can go to an automobile dealer (or its website) and order a vehicle to specification: model, power plant, color, and so on?

Well, what the Wolfsburg plant is able to do is put automobiles together by model, color, trim, engine, and so on—all different brands—ALL ON THE SAME ASSEMBLY LINE! You could see the robots build an Audi sedan, a VW Atlas, or a Tiguan, one after another on the production line!

Programming—coordinating the activity on an assembly line to produce one "copy"—is one thing; to do what the Wolfsburg plant does is just this side of a miracle.

Astonishing as it is, it is child's play in comparison to the human brain.

Let's break down the process just a bit more. This might stretch *your* brain, but picture a single human being standing outside the Wolfsburg plant. Each entity (the human being and the factory) possesses the ability to think. The human being's intelligence is part of its physical makeup; the factory must receive signals from somewhere in order to carry out its assigned tasks. These signals come in the form of digital code.

Each "control room" (factory or brain) receives input as to what action or "ideation" is needed in a particular situation. The human being might get a signal saying, "I'm hungry; let's go get a tuna sandwich." They go to a corner, buy the sandwich and some chips, a pickle, eat, then perhaps take a nap.

The Wolfsburg plant's control room receives input to produce a VW Tiguan, light blue, tan interior, battery-powered (EV), stereo package, and third-row seating. Then it communicates what is required to the production floor. The plant and the human being then deploy the robots or anatomical component parts as needed to accomplish their specific purposes. The sandwich has to get digested, move into the large intestine...

Think again about what is required to produce that Tiguan. What if it is preceded on the assembly line by a bright-red VW Jetta? Then a green VW Taos is right behind it on the line? Help!

Clearly, on the automobile production line, there is a massive need for *coordination.* Components and human interventions need to be ready for deployment; someone needs to tell those robots what the heck they're supposed to do. Once the tuna sandwich and that pickle get swallowed, the digestive system pretty much takes over and finishes off the process (although, let's not even get started on additional organs, chemicals, enzymes...).

To put this in highly technical language, each processing operation (car manufacture, sandwich eating) requires a boatload of *coordination.* And now we're back to the human brain and how it works.

We are going to learn more about trauma and the way our bodies (including our brains) deal with it. A traumatizing event can have a severe impact, but the body's reaction to it is the same as it is for other phenomena: identification, action, result. The "action" part includes the assignment of discrete functions to different parts of our nervous system, including those housed in these amazing organs occupying our crania—our brains.

There are "instructional" needs for specific actions (e.g., kicking a football), and also the planning/*sequencing* of different components and systems. Something has to coordinate the resulting activity.

Enter the Networks

This is from the Mindantics people (2018). They allege that "...the ability to think creatively depends on the interconnectedness between different parts of the brain involved in creative problem solving" (para. 4). (Please underline "interconnectedness.")

The three parts or neural networks are:

- **Default network**: This network includes the cortical midline and posterior inferior parietal regions of the brain. The default network is active when you are not in deliberate thought and helps in idea generation (para. 5).
- **Executive network**: This network is composed of the anterior and lateral regions of the prefrontal cortex and other interconnected regions, and is activated when you are consciously thinking; it has responsibility for

planning, reasoning, and decision-making (para. 6).

- **Salience network**: The salience network comprises bilateral insula and anterior cingulate cortex; it facilitates the transition between the default and executive networks. An insula, in addition to being a person's name (or is that "Ursula"?) is a collection of convolutions under the lateral dividing line of the brain (para. 7).

Let me try to put the foregoing in more familiar terms, and, in the process, explain its relevance to our topic (PTSD and C-PTSD). When you are simply relaxing on your couch, the *default* network of your brain guides you to simple tasks such as turning on the air conditioning, popping the popcorn, finding the appropriate TV channel. It's the grazin' in the grass mode.

When you suddenly realize that your company's monthly financial report is due the next day, the *executive* network switches on, directing you to your files, finding the right spreadsheets, making sure that all numbers have been recorded.

The *salience* network is the coordinator and prioritizer, the master computer in the Wolfsburg plant. *In human beings, the salience network is the controller that can get knocked out of whack by trauma.* This can be manifested in something called *emotional dysregulation.*

Emotional Dysregulation

"Dysregulation" means the absence, distortion, or minimization of regulatory control. Dibdin (2022) tells us that "emotional dysregulation, also called 'affect dysregulation,' describes difficulty with processing or regulating emotional responses. It can involve experiencing intense sadness, anger, or anxiety that feel difficult to control" (para. 8).

She adds the following possible symptoms (i.e., What does emotional dysregulation look like?):

- abrupt shifts in mood
- crying for no apparent reason
- inability to calm down or finding it difficult to soothe yourself
- intense or disproportionate emotional symptoms that are hard to control
- feeling easily overwhelmed by your emotions
- having difficulty coping with stress
- engaging in impulsive behavior
- displaying outbursts of anger
- misusing substances (para. 9)

Dibdin tells us that some people with emotional dysregulation may diagnose as depressed, anxious, or both. These mental health conditions often occur together (para. 10).

Distorted Self-Concept

Since we've gone from Rock Hudson movies to automobile manufacturing, let's remind ourselves of where we are here in Chapter 2. We are looking at ways that PTSD and C-PTSD affect the ways we conduct our lives and our relationships with others, along with the neuro-psychological machinery that affects both. An important outcome of the disorders can be strange ways of "seeing" ourselves; we're about to learn that the images that we send to our own psyches can be far different from the living, breathing realities.

In your lifetime, you may have met someone who seemed to be often preoccupied with their appearance. Too preoccupied, you might think, given other factors that require attention (such as work, education, family, job performance, and so on).

This can start early in life. Children, especially when allowed to run amok, can be extremely cruel, focusing on things like size, body shape, hair color, complexion —any way that they can place one another lower on the group status ladder. I was walking in our neighborhood one day (I may have been ten years old), when my friend Ronni's mother yelled at me, "They have rubber hoses at school that they use on children like you!"

Ouch! Where did *that* come from? It came from Ronni telling her mother that I called her "Fatty," "Chubby," and any number of unflattering names pertaining to her size. I was duly chastised (and terrified), and never again called Ronni anything other than her given name. Shame on me, perhaps especially because, like Ronni, I myself hadn't placed high in any beauty competitions.

So we develop these disproportionate, inaccurate images of ourselves, and we can reach the conclusion that others are "seeing" the same thing we are. This can actually lead to a condition called body dysmorphic disorder, or BDD.

The helpful practitioners at the EZ Care Clinic (2022) provide the following symptoms of a distorted self-concept:

- Avoiding mirrors to avoid seeing the whole body or the part of the body that is deemed unattractive.
- Trying to cover up the whole body (e.g., with baggy clothes or with accessories such as hats and caps to hide specific body parts.)
- Repeatedly inquiring of others how you look.

- Exaggerating how the body or a specific part of it looks with excessive makeup or even surgical procedures.
- Frequent fussing with grooming or style.
- Avoiding social interaction due to a person believing they look terrible and are feeling extremely self-conscious.
- Feeling depressed, which may lead to self-harming and even thoughts of suicide. (para. 10)

According to the professionals at Johns Hopkins Medicine-Health (n.d.), "Body dysmorphic disorder (BDD) is indeed a mental health problem. With BDD, you may be so appalled at the appearance of your body that it interferes with your ability to live anything like a normal life. Many of us *imagine* flaws in our appearance, but with BDD, our reactions to these "flaws" may become disproportionate and overwhelming" (para. 1).

The Johns Hopkins people further allege that thinking about our bodies in this manner can be hard to control. Those suffering from this disorder may spend hours *daily* worrying about how they look. If left untreated, as stated in the bulleted list above, in some cases it can lead to suicide. (para. 2)

When symptoms become severe, Hopkins Medical suggests getting psychiatric help and following these guidelines:

- Know why you're seeking help and what outcomes you hope for.
- Write down the questions you want answered.
- Bring someone with you to assist with questions and to record what your provider tells you.
- Write down the name of new diagnoses, and any new medicines, treatments, or tests. Include any new instructions your provider gives you. (Often providers will supply a printout with all of this information.)
- Understand why a new medicine or treatment is prescribed, and how it will do for you. Ask what side effects might be and how they can be handled. Ask if your condition can be treated in alternative ways.
- Know why a test or procedure is recommended and what results could mean.
- Know what to expect if you fail to take medications or have the test or procedure.
- Write down the date, time, and reason for your next visit.

- Know contact details for your provider should you have questions. (para. 15)

A personal note? If you're like me, you may want to race out of the doctor's office as quickly as you can once you've had your visit. Try to resist this impulse. The doctor is there for you, not the other way around. You are the customer. You need information and you shouldn't be shy about asking for it. When you visit your dentist, disregard all of the foregoing. Get out of there with all speed.

Dissociation

We discussed dissociation earlier, but we need to review it again in light of our current emphasis: looking more closely at the impact of PTSD and C-PTSD and what can be done to lessen that impact.

Nowak (2019) reminds us of the "staying power" of our responses to trauma. Of these experiences, she says that they can be too much for someone to process. This can lead to their carrying unresolved pain with them. Apparently many triggers—related or unrelated—can be reminders and stir up "lingering trauma." Even in the absence of an immediate threat, Nowak says that individuals can "experience nightmares, flashbacks, and other forms of overwhelming anxiety" (para. 4).

Remember that with complex PTSD, this kind of suffering is intensified. Nowak reminds us that C-PTSD is our mind's way of trying to protect ourselves from trauma. Somehow a person's consciousness shuts down to block the intensity of the trauma. What the person is doing, Nowak tells us, is, "...'burying' responses to trauma, and means must be discovered to dig it up and face it" (para. 5).

Memory can be affected. Trauma survivors may feel detached from their surroundings and their actions. They may experience gaps in their memory surrounding the traumatizing event or even regarding a normal, everyday task: "...they may feel out of touch with their own grounded identity" (para. 6).

In thinking about PTSD and C-PTSD, I'm reminded of Scott Peck's book, *The Road Less Traveled*, and its famous first words, "Life is difficult." In his book he discusses our reluctance to delay gratification, preferring immediate comfort to longer-lasting solutions to our problems. For many issues, like rivers that must be crossed, sometimes there's nothing for it but to dive in: experience the cold, the current, the rocks, and the snags; warmth and secure footing can be waiting on the other side.

Complex PTSD and the Attachment Theory

We are all on a continuing journey of self-discovery, every mother's son and daughter of us. Part of this journey involves the willingness to go back to our roots, as it were, to see if we can discover how early childhood experiences may be affecting us in the present. Heaven forbid that we discover some early trouble/trauma that continues to affect us on our journeys to adulthood.

Early childhood experiences are vital to our development, both physical and psychological. What concerns us here is how these experiences may be affecting us in adulthood, especially the ways they impact our relationships with others. Being the social creatures that we are, it's vital that we learn to interact successfully with other people.

It's bad enough that trauma occurs to some of us later in life, but it's all the more serious if that trauma is preceded by developmental issues from very early in our lives. Scholars and medical people have evolved something called "attachment theories" to explain the ways we learn to interact with our fellow creatures.

Supposedly, there are four primary ways that we connect or sometimes fail to connect with them:

- secure
- avoidant
- anxious
- disorganized

Simply put, if we receive warm, supportive care early on, we are very likely to be able to relate warmly and supportively toward others later in life. We form secure attachments. If not, we may tend to avoid, be anxious about, or find ourselves all over the place in relationships as adults.

This information is available from Therapy Cincinnati (2021), which explains how an insecure attachment style can result from a traumatic relationship. A person with this attachment style may also exhibit Complex PTSD. "...something that repeatedly occurred or else happened over a long period of time can come alive in the present moment. Experiencing an unhealthy relationship where continuous trauma was experienced can lead to Complex PTSD Attachment Style" (para. 3).

They add that if we find ourselves avoiding commitment, intimacy, or deep connections, or if relationships cause us intense anxiety and distress, we may have Complex PTSD Attachment Style. (para. 4)

The problematic attachment styles (avoidant, anxious, disorganized) can be treated with a number of different therapies, the most prominent of these being cognitive restructuring. "Cognition" means "thinking," so this therapeutic approach sets out to change the way you think. Cognitive restructuring is most effectively administered by a trained therapist, one who will guide you back to and through the experiences that led to your current way of thinking.

Impairment in Functioning

It should be clear by now that PTSD/C-PTSD can have a considerable effect on an individual's day-to-day functioning. The Better Health Channel people (n.d.) remind us of the following.

Most of us work, do the mundane activities needed to sustain ourselves (visit the doctor, grocery shop, get our hair cut). PTSD and C-PTSD can throw wrenches into any and all of these. With these disorders, we can seem uninterested or withdrawn, seeming detached from even those closest to us. Of course our significant others can feel "shut out" of their prior associations with us when this happens. (para. 10)

These "shutting out" behaviors only add to the problem. Those struggling with PTSD or C-PTSD need the support of family, friends, and co-workers, but may inadvertently push them away. A lack of understanding of what they're going through can keep them from getting the support they need. (para. 11)

And one thing can lead to another. According to The Better Health Channel (n.d.), up to 80 percent of people afflicted with PTSD or C-PTSD develop other mental health issues such as depression, anxiety, alcohol and other substance abuse. These other factors may be traced back to traumatizing events or the effects of *having* PTSD (para. 12).

I like the phrase "How's that working for you?" It can almost force a person who is clearly not dealing well with something to explore both what they are going through and how well they're dealing with it. Ask this of yourself if you're having the kinds of issues discussed here; ask it of a friend, partner, or coworker who is clearly struggling.

C-PTSD and Borderline Personality Disorder (BPD)

People struggling with borderline personality disorder (BPD) have boatloads of issues ("boatload" is a technical term meaning "a lot"). Tanasugarn (2020) describes the condition as a pervasive and lifelong mental disorder, one that can affect interpersonal relationships, mood, and behavior. Those with BPD can struggle with a rickety self-identity and self-image. They can have difficulty regulating their emotions, engaging in impulsive and self-sabotaging behavior. They can also exhibit a fear of being abandoned, develop feelings of emptiness, and engage in a pattern of highly unstable relationships. (para. 1).

Tanasugarn believes that C-PTSD is actually a subset of PTSD. While PTSD is a fear-based disorder, C-PTSD can be referred to as a "shame-based disorder," one originating from chronic and long-term exposure to traumatic events such as continuing, severe child abuse or long-term relationship abuse. (para. 3)

Those having experienced repeated trauma very early in life are at a greater risk for developing C-PTSD, such as children who cannot escape their home environments. Their symptoms can include "...flashbacks of the events, fear, despair, shame, chronic devaluation of self, terror, and avoidance of socialization or relationships." Apparently those who have experienced severe, ongoing trauma in childhood are at greater risk for being *re-traumatized* in adulthood—especially in romantic relationships. This increases their risk of developing C-PTSD or a worsening of existing symptoms (para. 3).

Not to oversimplify, but it does sound like the three disorders (PTSD, C-PTSD, BPD) are peas in the same psychiatric pod. My primary takeaway is that BPD can emerge from some of the same experiences as PTSD and C-PTSD, but it can also emerge from inherited dispositions not easily cataloged.

Most of us have few issues with seeing experts for various conditions: cardiologists for our hearts; oncologists for cancer; dermatologists for skin problems; podiatrists for our feet. I am often impressed with the skills and knowledge that characterize these specialists. Just as we can have issues with any bodily organ, structure or system, specialists are out there who can help us with our emotional/mental functioning, and there should be no stigma attached to this. They have a raft of techniques, approaches and therapies to apply to our specific situations, among them something called cognitive behavioral therapy or CBT.

We'd best have a careful look at that in Chapter 3.

3

COGNITIVE BEHAVIORAL
THERAPY (CBT)

HARD REALITIES

Earlier in life, I had a relationship with someone that I thought would go on forever. It did not. At the time I was even better at displaying abject misery than I am now, which is really saying something. I moped around about this for a pretty good while. After whining about it yet again to a good friend, she told me, "You've got to get over this! You're yesterday's news!"

Something in that last sentence clicked. One thing was the slap-in-the-face directness of her remark: your standard cold-water-in-the-face effect. It opened my eyes. I was able to see the situation more clearly, and, importantly, to begin to move past my earlier reactions to it. Do you know the dining room trick, where an individual takes hold of a tablecloth at one end of the table, then gives it a sudden yank, leaving the dishes and food where they were? Sometimes we simply have to let the past crash to the floor like a table full of dishes and cold food.

School Daze

Early in my teaching career, I taught English to a group of under-achieving high school students. Two boys in the class gave me a particularly bad time. My efforts to get them in line had proven to be ineffectual, so I asked my department chair, since he had a similar class meeting at the same time, if I could swap my two miscreants for two of his students.

I did this for a considerable period of time, but my department chair would not give me a clear answer to my repeated pleas for help. Finally, after one particularly moving entreaty, he said. "Sure."

Relief swept over me! Free at last!

Then he said, "I'll be happy to take responsibility for your mistakes."

Initially stunned, I paused, then went to the class and dealt with my two malcontents. They were to select me for elective classes throughout the rest of their checkered high school careers. I had to learn that I was not

COMPLEX PTSD RECOVERY: | 61

teaching at Eton or Cambridge. In public school, you deal with the hands you're dealt.

It sounds so simple, but in both of these instances I had to *change the way I was thinking*. My "ideation," my thought process, had led me to some maladaptive, ineffective behavior. To set me straight, others had to hold a mirror up for me to peer into, one that gave me a clearer idea of how I was thinking, and the impact that was having on my life and career.

COGNITIVE BEHAVIORAL THERAPY (CBT)

The Society of Clinical Psychology (2017) alleges that cognitive behavioral therapy (CBT) has quite a record of success: "Numerous research studies suggest that CBT leads to significant improvement in functioning and quality of life... CBT has been demonstrated to be as effective as, or more effective than, other forms of psychological therapy or psychiatric medications" (para. 1).

The core principles of CBT are these:

- Psychological problems are based partly on faulty or unhelpful ways of thinking.
- Psychological problems are based partly on learned patterns of unhelpful behavior.

- People suffering from psychological problems can learn better ways of handling them, in the process relieving symptoms and becoming more effective in their lives (para. 3).

While the examples from my own life may not exhibit actual pathology (my friends and workmates might disagree), they do illustrate the three principles just listed. What I had to do, again according to the SCP, was face and deal with the situations I found myself in; I had to calm down; I could have role-played or employed other tactics designed to help me "face the music" (para. 5).

CBT, through exercises in therapy sessions as well as "homework" exercises outside of them, patients are helped to develop coping skills, then learn to *change their own thinking, problematic emotions, and behavior.* (para. 6)

CBT is forward-looking. Some background information is required, but the emphasis in CBT is on the here and now (My question, "How's that working for you?" rings in my mind).

Different Kinds of Cognitive Behavioral Therapy

Cherry (2022) reminds us that CBT includes a range of techniques and approaches that can address our thoughts, emotions, and behaviors, from structured psychotherapies to self-help practices. Some approaches include:

- *Cognitive therapy* includes identifying and changing inaccurate or distorted thought habits, emotional responses, and behaviors.
- *Dialectical behavior therapy (DBT)* incorporates a focus on destructive or disturbing thoughts and behaviors; it uses treatment strategies such as emotional regulation and mindfulness.
- *Multimodal therapy* suggests that psychological issues must be treated by addressing seven different but related "modalities": behavior, affect, sensation, imagery, cognition, interpersonal factors, and drug/biological considerations. (Remember that "affect" refers to the degrees that emotion is shown.)
- *Rational emotive behavior therapy (REBT)* uncovers irrational beliefs, actively challenges them, and initiates lessons in recognizing and changing them (para. 5).

In the second bullet above, the critical word is "dialectical." You of course recognize the prefix "dia." That prefix means "across," as in the word "diaphragm," which refers to the large lateral muscle extending across our abdomens, and "diameter," which divides a circle in two. My unprofessional definition of "dialectical" in the therapeutic context is that it addresses the bridge from problematic thoughts and behaviors to more healthful alternatives.

Core Concepts of CBT

Forgive me, but I forget where this next idea came from (I could have, in fact, invented it). It refers, of course, to cognitive behavioral therapy. What I want to emphasize is the sheer practicality of CBT as a therapy option. The idea is that we can accomplish "a sudden reorganization of conceptual space." In practical language, that means that we can learn to think differently. Different thinking can lead to new, more productive and satisfying modes of behavior.

As much as I admire Dr. Scott Peck and his pioneering book *The Road Less Traveled*, the therapy experiences he describes seem to take a very long time, as in months and years. To make a clumsy analogy, if we get a flat tire on our car, we don't sit down and think: "Hmmmm. I don't know how this happened, but I'd best conceive of and construct a new rubber device to fit on this rim. I'll go to South America, find a rubber plantation, select plants ripe to be harvested…" You get the idea.

I don't know if they still do this, but for a time, car manufacturers would put tiny little tires in the trunks of cars to be used as spares. You'd put one of these little donuts on your car, wobble to a tire store, and either get the damaged tire repaired or buy a new one.

The little spare tire would allow you to function until a new tire could make the car "whole" again. Please don't make me spell out this analogy to CBT. Oh, alright. CBT proposes a solution that you can employ quickly. Of course, it won't transform you immediately, but it can address the current problem to a degree (put the donut on the car). It can get you to the nearest tire store where a more satisfactory solution can be found.

Referencing the American Psychological Association, Raypole and Marcin (2023) outline for us the key concepts of CBT. These two worthies allege that psychological issues are in part based on "unhelpful ways of thinking and learned patterns of behavior," and that people living with this kind of thinking and this kind of behavior "can improve with better coping mechanisms and management to help relieve their symptoms" (para 8).

Our authors provide a "closer look at how thoughts and emotions can influence behavior—in a positive or negative way":

- Distorted/inaccurate/negative perceptions or ideas can lead to emotional distress and to mental health concerns.
- These lead to inappropriate, maladaptive behaviors.
- These behaviors can form a repeating pattern.
- Learning to confront and deal with maladaptive patterns early reduces the probability that they will repeat themselves (para. 9).

Thus: Perception > Behavior > Pattern > Confrontation/Remediation. Since you're a Shakespearean scholar, I know you recall the Duke of Kent saying to the aging, more-and-more irrational King, "See better Lear!" (1606). He (Lear) didn't, which led to the events and eventual heart-rending tragedy of that play. CBT starts people on the path to "seeing better" and the resulting benefits that can accrue from that.

Frame of Reference

Let me say another word about the opening item of our experts' list, *perception*. We perceive things through our own peculiar *frame of reference*. By "peculiar" I don't mean "odd," I just mean unique: Each of us views the world through the lens of our individual experience.

A quick example. A work colleague of mine, years ago, went through a particularly painful divorce. She was blindsided by her husband's decision that he no longer wanted to be married to her. Her divorce had occurred some ten years before I met her, but the divorce seemed to affect her as strongly in the present as it had a decade earlier. She literally couldn't see past it.

Multiply this experience by all the other experiences of her life, positive and negative, and you have the composite "frame of reference" through which she processed things: through which and with which she "colored" the events of her life. Of course I don't remember this personally (how old do you think I *am?*), but I understand there was a song years ago called "Aquarius," sung by the Fifth Dimension, in which they intoned "Let the sunshine in!" My divorced coworker never learned to do this, at least during the time I worked with her. A shame.

Photographers know all about putting different lenses on cameras for different purposes: close-up for close up, telephoto for far away, wide-angle to get as much into the frame as they can. There may be a lesson there for our own perceiving devices. We'll see. I think I want that telephoto on the camera as often as I can get it. If I can keep people and events far away, they won't be able to get me...

CBT and PTSD

The people at Posttraumatic Stress Disorder (2017) recount the story of an Iraq War veteran who was treated successfully with CBT (first reported by Monson and Schnaider, 2014).

The veteran, whose name is Jill, was driving a supply truck at the head of a convoy of other vehicles during the war. Her vehicle experienced a malfunction, and she had to pull off to the side of the road. She waved the next vehicle in line past. The driver of the second vehicle, a soldier named Mike, and his friends made jokes about Jill and her "wreck" of a vehicle as they moved past her (she and her companions had already begun working to get her vehicle moving again).

Two hundred yards past Jill's vehicle, Mike's truck hit an IED (improvised explosive device) and was blown up, with soldiers in Mike's truck being killed in the explosion. Jill blamed herself for their deaths, thinking that had she not pulled off the road, the rest of the convoy might have escaped harm. She suffered severe PTSD symptoms for five years after the incident before undergoing CBT.

In therapy, she was led to rethink the entire episode. Her therapist helped her see that there was no way anyone could have seen the IED at all, let alone at a distance of two hundred yards. Second, the therapist asked her what the standard procedure (protocol) was in an instance like the one she'd experienced. She replied that in an instance like this one, the protocol was to keep the convoy moving, lest it become an easier target for enemy fire.

The operative word here is "rethink," and subsequently make a more positive evaluation of one's participation in a traumatic event.

Cognitive Processing Therapy (CPT) for Prolonged Exposure

Thailand is home to a lot of monkeys. Don't test me on this, but I've read of locations in that country where troops of monkeys are extremely aggressive, accosting humans in search of food (I hope that's all they're after).

I'm not fond of monkeys as a species, and this is one reason I'm not contemplating a future trip to Thailand, with finances being a secondary reason. If I go abroad at all, perhaps I'll go to Iceland to have a look at those volcanoes.

To return to the monkeys, the treatment for PTSD we're looking at in this section is Cognitive Processing Therapy, or CPT. In this process, PTSD patients are guided through a number of experiences to gradually reduce their discomfort and/or anxiety about them.

The people at Posttraumatic Stress Disorder (2020) allege that, "Most people want to avoid anything that reminds them of the trauma they experienced" (para. 3). I can certainly relate to that, but as the PTSD people remind us, avoidance like this is counterproductive.

I think about this concept when I consider learning how to swim. I have a nephew who, as a very young child, was terrified of going in the water. It would have been very disturbing to him, to say the least, to be tossed into a lake, for example, or perhaps off of a dock. The thing his understanding parents did was take him *to* the water (lakes, pools, beaches), but allow him to venture into the water when, how, and on what terms he would do so (e.g., holding someone's hand or being carried). After any number of these occasions, his fear lessened and he was able to enjoy the water with the rest of his family.

Let's return to my potential monkey phobia (in fact it isn't "potential"; it's quite real). If this had a truly maladaptive influence on my life, I could begin CPT to address it. I might discuss my fear with a caregiver (preferably a trained therapist), mentioning where I thought the fear might have originated.

Our experts allege that it could take eight to ten sessions with a therapist to get a better grip on my monkey phobia. The therapeutic approach would thus be a very gradual one. Perhaps it would begin with brief discussions of my prior experiences with my fellow primates. I'm guessing, but later sessions could progress to looking at pictures and talking about how they made me feel. Later still, the therapist could show me brief video segments. Later still, I might make visits to zoos and view actual monkeys at a safe distance, gradually increasing the time I spent doing this.

I doubt that I would ever get a *pet* monkey, but one never knows.

Once again, the therapeutic process would begin with imagined, hypothetical considerations of the feared phenomenon, then proceed to what are called "in vivo" exposures. I don't know why the experts don't just call these "live" exposures, but they don't. These would be the lengthening visits I might make to the zoo, where I could view monkeys from a safe distance.

To test your grasp of this concept, think of something that truly scares you, and imagine how you might try the technique just described to get past that fear. Snakes. It would take a battalion of therapists and years of discussion to get me past that fear. The irony is, when I was a child, my brother and I lived near a large field which bordered some woods. The field was alive with garter snakes. We would catch them by the dozens and put them in jars. My brother once fell off a log into a nest of them, and I can still see them surrounding and crawling over him. Wait there while I find a therapist.

Trauma-Based CBT Principles

From Psychologytoday (2022) we hear the following about trauma-based CBT principles. They tell us that the approach originated in the 1990s through the efforts of psychiatrist Judith Cohen, along with psychologists Esther Deblinger and Anthony Mannarino. These people set out to observe children and adolescents who had experienced sexual abuse. TB-CBT has expanded over the years to include services for youths who have experienced many different forms of severe trauma or abuse (para. 2).

The method features combining theories and techniques of several therapeutic interventions. "By doing so, TB-CBT can address and improve the symptoms of post-traumatic stress in youth" (Psychologytoday, 2022). Core features can incorporate:

- *Psychoeducation* teaches patients about the normal reactions to traumatic experiences, reducing feelings of guilt or blame for what happened.
- *Coping skills* include relaxation exercises like deep breathing, mindfulness, acceptance, identifying and redirecting thoughts.

- *Gradual exposure* gradually introduces the patient to memories of their traumatic experience, reconditioning their responses to triggers and easing emotional distress.
- *Cognitive processing* means developing skills to recontextualize (rethink) unhelpful feelings and thoughts and to regulate emotions.
- *Caregiver involvement* can include rebuilding trusting adult relationships for the child and also training the caregiver in how to best be a resource for the child (para. 10).

CBT Worksheets

Experts tell us that writing down goals increases the chance that we will achieve the goals by some 80 percent. Good odds, by anyone's standard.

Among their most ardent proponents is Stephen Covey, he of *7 Habits* fame. Pick up your copy of the book right now, and turn to pages 180–181. There you'll see a chart called THE WEEKLY SCHEDULE, and on it he has categories for Roles, Goals, Priorities, Appointments, and Commitments.

Most of us don't spend a lot of time thinking about "roles," but Covey does, and thinking about roles can help us focus on both what we do and who is involved in our various activities. I've seen that troubled people can spend a great deal of time, as the saying goes, "stewing in their juices." Regardless of the kinds of therapies they may try, a valuable adjunct to any of them is keeping a record; whether it is as involved as Covey's or not, the main thing is to simply *do* one. It gives both structure and visibility to our efforts to get better.

There are literally dozens of worksheets available online for charting various therapeutic activities. In addition to these I recommend journaling.

Elsewhere in his book Covey tells us that we love to tell our own stories, and I believe this is true, even of the most reclusive and shy of us. Yes, I personally am shy and reclusive, going outside only in the dead of night. I have been a journaler.

The journaling process can be both freeing and illuminating . The old saying is, "How do I know what I think until I see what I say?" This applies, of course, to the patient-therapist relationship as well as journaling. If you do this, don't edit yourself, but let thoughts emerge freely.

Whether via worksheets, journaling, or other means, do something to make your therapeutic efforts concrete.

Wow. Next we have to talk about "Dialectical Behavioral Therapy," or DBT. "Buckle up," as the saying goes.

4

DIALECTICAL BEHAVIORAL THERAPY

PERSONALITY DISORDERS AND THE LAW

I want to begin this chapter with a brief discussion of stigma and discrimination. "Stigma" refers to a set of negative beliefs about something or someone, often without solid empirical or scientific evidence. I, for example, attach stigma unfairly to all pitbulls. Don't tell me they're kind, faithful, and trustworthy. I know so much better.

To discriminate, in the sense I'll use the term, means "to set apart because of a perceived difference." I'll use an example from my storied career in Human Resources. Suppose you're an HR person charged with recruiting. You have an opening in your company for a warehouse worker. One of the tasks related to the position is using a ladder regularly to retrieve parts on high shelves.

You select a half-dozen candidates from your applicant pool to interview. One candidate is a young woman named Martha. On the day of her interview, Martha arrives and it is immediately apparent that she has lost part of her right leg, just above the knee. As the consummate professional you are, dedicated to ensuring the rights of all applicants under the law, you conduct the first part of the interview asking Martha the same questions you've asked other applicants.

As the interview draws to a close, you decide to ask Martha about her leg. You phrase your question this way: "Part of this job involves going up and down a ladder to retrieve parts and packages; do you think you would have any trouble doing that?" Martha replies "Absolutely not!"

You are allowed under the law to ask her, "Would you mind showing me?"

Martha says she would be happy to show you. You accompany her to the warehouse, locate a ladder, and ask her to climb it. She does so with speed and skill. You thank her and say you'll be in touch after interviewing the rest of your candidate pool.

And speaking of that candidate pool, guess what you now have to do with each one of them? That's correct. You have to take each of them to the warehouse and ask them to climb the ladder.

The hiring situation is only one area in which discrimination can occur in the workplace. It is not uncommon for individuals with mental/behavioral disorders to be involved in disciplinary matters. In these instances, employers can focus simply on actions and not underlying causes/reasons for those actions, leading to increased discipline up to and including termination.

This is simply a request for you, should you have a role in anything like the examples just discussed, to at least take a pause and a longer look at what might be affecting an individual having behavioral issues at work. It is estimated that as many as one in five people in the workplace display personality or behavioral issues that require treatment. If you have a voice in ensuring equal treatment (both from therapeutic and legal standpoints), help the 20 percent get the treatment they need.

DIALECTICAL BEHAVIOR THERAPY

Last night for dinner, one item on the menu was stewed tomatoes. I know, right? Who in their right mind likes stewed tomatoes?

I finished off my shrimp mac and cheese, then looked again at my helping of stewed tomatoes. Seeing nothing else on my plate to engage my attention, I gingerly speared a forkful of tomato (the helping was pre-cut into bite-sized chunks) and put it in my mouth. To my astonishment, the bite was delicious, and I quickly ate the remainder that was on my plate.

Pay close attention here: *The experience taught me the importance of re-thinking formerly accepted "truths" about things.*

For those who struggle with PTSD and borderline personality disorder (BPD), rethinking is exactly what they need to do. In each case, according to Tull (2020) individuals can display difficulty managing emotions, interpersonal problems and/or experience a high risk of impulsive behavior (para. 3)

Tull provides a closer look at cognitive behavioral therapy (CBT), which is centered on "changing poorly formed thoughts, behaviors, and beliefs as a way of reducing a person's BPD symptoms." CBT places greater emphasis on "acceptance of the person's emotions and thoughts." Increasing mindfulness is one development of engaging in CBT (para. 4). I know you never forget anything, but remember that mindfulness means paying hard attention to the here and now, versus thoughts and images from the past. The latter can develop a patina that is hard to see through.

I'm going to borrow information now from a rather folksy Ph.D specialist named Kirby Reutter (2022) to help us get a firmer grasp of dialectical behavioral therapy. Dr. Reutter supplies the following:

- Dialectics has to do with restoring balance and finding the middle path between extremes.
- DBT incorporates five main skill sets: mindfulness, distress tolerance, emotion regulation, dialectical thinking, and interpersonal effectiveness.
- Trauma-focused DBT, or TF-DBT, is a form of standard DBT, designed to treat symptoms of trauma.
- DBT helps clients get out of hell and build a life worth living through skills work (para. 1).

Characterizing Dr. Reutter's style as "folksy," I refer to expressions such as "get out of hell." Perhaps I should use the word "casual" instead; he's trying to get us to relax. He begins by helping us with a definition of "dialectics," a term borrowed from philosophy, and it basically refers to bringing together opposites. Dialectics has to do with looking at things from new or different perspectives (para. 4).

Dialectics incorporates the idea that two seemingly antithetical phenomena can both be true at the same time. Reutter refers to work done by one Marsha Linehan called the "bio-social theory," which alleges that both biological and social/environmental factors can be involved in BPD (para. 5). In other words, we can be psychologically inclined in a given direction (such as Eeyore's mopy orientation in the Winnie the Pooh stories), and also be subject to the influence of our environment. Living in squalor would likely affect us differently than living in palatial splendor.

As if we don't have enough complex terminology to grasp in studying our "psycho-social" functioning, Reutter somewhat cavalierly introduces the concept of "temperament." He first says that temperament refers to our personality *style*, then gives us some examples.

One is a very sensitive temperament. Another is just a high-maintenance temperament, a temperament that's perhaps more difficult to deal with. And the third temperament actually isn't even a specific kind of temperament. It's just any temperament that Reutter calls an "outlier," very different from any other temperament within the family (para. 6).

As for high-maintenance, of course you've known people you'd characterize in this manner. I always think of cars when I hear the phrase "high-maintenance." In that context, the phrase means that you have to pay a lot of attention to various features and systems to ensure that a vehicle performs as it should. You have to change the oil every hundred yards or so; you have to top off fluids every ten blocks; you have to ensure tire pressure stays within tight psi (pounds per square inch) or risk losing control of the vehicle.

Reutter's third kind of temperament is kind of blurry: "...any temperament... just very different from any other temperament within the family." I guess if you were, for example, a cerebral, reserved, bookish person in a family of athletic extroverts, this quality could apply to you. Young Sheldon on the TV program that bears his name is typical, except he appears to *cause* more trauma than he develops in his beleaguered parents and siblings.

The Main Modules of CBT

"Modules" is a strange word for this new sub-topic, in that the different considerations of CBT are not uniform, but I am nothing if not obedient and conformative to the therapeutic community, so "modules" it is. I would have used "areas" instead of "modules," since I believe it to be more accurate.

I've actually engaged the DBT Skills Group of New Jersey (2023) to learn more about four considerations (modules) of CBT useful for those dealing with and/or increasing their awareness of this therapy model. These four areas are:

- core mindfulness
- distress tolerance
- emotion regulation
- interpersonal effectiveness (para. 1)

The Skills people allege that developing proclivities in the DBT areas listed will be useful in overcoming a variety of PTSD/C-PTSD symptoms. Doing so should "...help people who experience problems with anger or the expression of anger, episodic depression, irritability or anxiety, intense or chaotic relationships, impulsivity, stress, and feelings of emptiness" (para. 1).

Mindfulness has to do with mental focus, the ability to sustain our attention on a specific topic, the quality of being able to remain in the here and now. To achieve *distress tolerance,* people need to accept and adapt to current reality. *Emotion regulation* skills include learning to identify and label current emotions; identifying obstacles to changing them; reducing emotional reactivity; increasing positive emotions and changing emotions. *Interpersonal Effectiveness* skills inculcate "...strategies for asking for what one needs, saying no, and coping with interpersonal conflict" (para. 2).

Distress tolerance teaches people to soothe themselves in healthy ways when they are feeling upset rather than becoming overwhelmed by emotions or hiding from them. Doing so helps people make better decisions about whether and how to take action, (i.e., not falling into "intense, desperate, and often-destructive emotional reactions"). You remember the hole maxim, right? If you find yourself in one, stop digging?

Emotion regulation suggests that we can govern our emotions versus being governed by them. At first this seems counterintuitive: "Regulation" may seem more applicable to the realm of logic and reason, and these are often considered the opposite of emotion. Perhaps it's like hearing a train coming, but it's still out of sight? Hearing the sound of it can alert us to stay off the tracks until the train passes.

On this topic, let me apologize for suggesting that emotion and reason are totally distinct from each other, because they are not. I would think that taking a hard punch in a boxing ring could lead to a highly emotional response, as in "I've got to get the _____ out of here!" But the fighter taking the punch, in a shaken but logical response, says to themself, "If that's the best they've got, I'm in good shape here!"

Interpersonal skills serve us well in virtually every situation involving communication and cooperation with others. The Skills Group reminds us that such skills help us become aware of others' needs in relationships and to develop effective ways of dealing with them "to get one's wants or needs met in a healthy way."

A key element in this process is respect, both for ourselves and the others involved. We have to include dealing with difficult people in this context, sometimes a tall order—especially when we deal with those who have developed the ability to recognize and push our buttons (para. 5).

Of the four considerations just mentioned, one of them would seem to both overarch and infuse all of them, and that is mindfulness. PTSD and C-PTSD are phantoms of the mind; that's where they live, not in the real world of bicycles and mashed potatoes. Mindfulness brings us back to things we can see and touch; it "grounds" us. It's not unlike that bar that holds us in our seats on the roller coaster. I should say "holds *you*," because I have nothing to do with roller coasters. I like to sit at home on my couch.

Treatment Phases of DBT-PTSD

Himidian (2020) reminds us of the stages that therapy incorporates in the DBT treatment model.

The first stage incorporates "stabilization, safety, and coping." The therapist begins to understand what trauma symptoms are affecting an individual; how intense the symptoms are along with what "collateral damage" they are causing in the patient's life. Next, the therapist has to make assessments of what "sensorimotor" indicators are characteristic in a patient's traumatic behavior situation (i.e., they try to understand what the patient thinks and does when experiencing post-event trauma).

The goal of the first stage is to begin building coping skills such as mindfulness, grounding, and tolerating distress. The latter involves some informal exposure to trauma-related events (i.e., "bringing them to mind") (para. 2).

In the second stage, the ante, so to speak, is raised. The patient is exposed to trauma content (e.g., recollections of the traumatic experiences), but only when the therapist concludes that the patient is ready for such exposure. A therapy often introduced during Stage Two is called Eye Movement Desensitization and Reprocessing (EMDR).

From the EMDR *Institute* people we learn that EMDR incorporates a three-pronged approach: First, the past events that have laid the groundwork for dysfunction are processed, making new associative links to adaptive information. Second, the current circumstances that trigger distress are targeted, and internal and external triggers are demobilized. Third, imaginary templates of future events are introduced to help the client acquire the skills needed to adapt more successfully in the future (para. 2).

In EMDR, after the clinician has determined which memory to target first, they ask the client to hold different parts of the traumatic event or thought in mind, and to use their eyes to track the therapist's hand as it moves back and forth across their field of vision. "As this happens, internal associations arise and the clients begin to process the memory and disturbing feelings. When successful, the meaning of painful events is transformed on an emotional level" (para. 4).

In Stage Three, "we witness a reconnection to values and a person's sense of self, their relationships, and their communities" (para.4).

Treatment Effectiveness

Whether PTSD or other psychological difficulty, many suffering from trauma-related disorders simply want the bad feelings to go away. That is like putting all your chips on one roulette number (If you insist on doing this, at least put them all on one *color*; that way you'll have a better chance).

Research indicates that dialectical behavioral therapy (DBT) does indeed work. According to Anwar (2022), abundant research has shown the efficacy of DBT for PTSD, with some studies finding it superior to CBT in reducing symptoms of complex PTSD. Clinical trial results indicate that DBT-PTSD leads to a reduction of PTSD symptoms in 58% of women survivors of childhood abuse as opposed to 41% in those who were treated solely with CBT (para. 5).

She further tells us that other studies have looked at how effective DBT-PTSD is in treating adult survivors of childhood sexual abuse (CSA). Results from these studies again offer confirmation that DBT-PTSD can be effective at reducing or eliminating symptoms of CSA-PTSD (para. 6).

With apologies to Mr. Wesley, (he of "do all the good you can" fame), the matter isn't this simple, however much I like the idea of "doing all the good you can." The problem enters when we try to define the very abstract term "good." We recall elders finding switches and taking us to the woodshed and administering punishment, "for our own good." Actually, I probably needed more of these journeys to the woodshed than I received.

In critiques of any theory or rationale, we will find people taking any number of sides, and this is certainly true of commentaries I've discovered about Dialectical Behavior Therapy. I would think traditional psychotherapists would have a good deal of trouble with the theory. Their methods can occur in a variety of ways and over extended periods of time. To vastly oversimplify, the latter method allows patients to settle in and explore deeply with a trusted respondent. The theory would be that insights gained in this way have a better opportunity to "take hold" and become firmly ingrained, as opposed to what could be seen as the application of a thinner veneer (which some could attribute to DBT).

The bottom line is, I expect "nothing will come of nothing" (this is a line stolen from *King Lear*, 1606). We can all choose to "wait out" our lives, doing little or nothing to alleviate the discomfort and actual pain we're experiencing. I recommend reaching out. What is an example of this?—The person, having fallen off a cliff, finds a root to grab hold of—and there they hang. An individual appears above who proffers a hand; to grab the hand, the branch-holder has to let go.

I trust that you have decided against retreating and trying to alleviate traumatic psychological symptoms on your own, and I can only say, "Good for you." As for DBT and its potential to assist you, you have little to lose by trying it.

5

MINDFULNESS-BASED THERAPIES

WHAT IS MINDFULNESS THERAPY?

Well, here's some challenging information (it's from the dedicated souls at GoodTherapy, 2018). At present, the GTs tell us there is no universally accepted definition for "mindfulness." The word has proven hard to define because of differing beliefs as to what exactly "mindfulness" is, and because of differing opinions as to how to *achieve* mindfulness, different views about the *purpose* of it, and the challenge of describing it using medical and psychological terminology (para. 3).

Undaunted, the GoodTherapies go on to allege that Mindfulness may be fundamentally understood as the state in which we become more aware of our physical, mental, and emotional condition—in the present moment, without becoming judgmental (para. 4). Here's the tricky part: In this kind of therapy, people can pay attention (to things such as physical sensations, thoughts, and feelings), *without being influenced by them.* The result can be people controlling their thoughts instead of being controlled *by* those thoughts (para. 4).

Olivine (2022) places mindfulness therapy as a form of psychotherapy, or talk therapy, "...a conversation-based intervention provided by a trained mental health professional to assess, diagnose, and treat dysfunctional thought patterns and behaviors" (para. 3).

Included in Olivine's description of mindfulness is an awareness of thoughts, emotions, feelings, surroundings, and situations, including conversations with professionals, through which people develop greater awareness of their thoughts and their surroundings. This, in Olivine's view, "...helps them avoid destructive or automatic responses or habits" (para. 4).

This is a point we shouldn't miss, the business of "automatic responses or habits." Given the stimuli that bombard us on a more or less continuous basis, we rarely take the time or initiative to subject them to careful observation and analysis. Becoming more mindful apparently leads us out of this pattern of perceiving and responding. We need to disengage autopilot and parse perceptions more carefully. Hence the following section.

Maps and Territories

I've talked around the idea of maps and territories earlier, but I want to be more specific here, given our increased attention paid to mindfulness. This will involve the briefest of forays into what language is and how it works.

Language is code. It involves sending and receiving messages. We have a perception, formulate the words to express it, and send it off to a receiver. The receiver uses their own unique processing apparatus to decode what we've sent.

When those in the therapeutic community discuss these matters, they ask us to be sure, as receivers, that we are decoding another's messages correctly (in addition to the messages we send ourselves). Here is a test. I send you the word "democrat." You are now obliged to decode "democrat." Into your *territory* book you go, searching for "democrat."

Somewhat tragically, you find a whole raft of territories for "democrat," and some of them are not neutral, but accompanied by an emotional charge as well. Perhaps your blood pressure rises and your face turns beet red. Actually, I'm quite disappointed that you're having this reaction.

As a word, "democrat" rises near the top of the "abstraction ladder." When we speak of words being highly abstract, that means they have many possible territories, or "meanings." Many conversations between democrats and those espousing different political beliefs rarely get past the first rung of the ladder. The interlocutor (receiver) processes "democrat," triggering a number of what can be negative impressions and opinions. Typically, the conversation is not a long one.

This is the dynamic that operates within the therapeutic interaction. The therapist, of course, has their own "meanings" and attendant feelings for various words and phases. What they propose to discover are the meanings and feelings *you* have for them. If they're to help you, you will have to show your territories to them. *Then you explore with the therapist how it feels to live in the territory you occupy and with the maps you've used to navigate through it.* It could be that you have to move to another location; it could be that you have to devise new maps.

A child thinks that there's a monster hiding in their closet. To relieve the fear that this idea generates, the child has to look in the closet. In the therapeutic interaction, all of us take the therapist to the closet and have a look.

Brain Change

Studies have shown that mindfulness therapy involves more than wishful thinking. To wit, it can be demonstrated by changes that occur in our gray matter during this kind of therapy.

Congleton et.al. (2015) reports that the business world is "abuzz with mindfulness." But perhaps, she cautions, we haven't heard that the hype is backed by what she calls "hard science." She tells us that research is providing strong evidence that practicing "non-judgmental, present-moment awareness" (a.k.a., mindfulness) changes our brains, and it "does so in ways that anyone working in today's complex business environment, and certainly every leader, should know about" (para. 1).

We're going to tread ever-so-carefully into the weeds of this research (the following is again from Congleton and her colleagues):

They delve first of all into the functioning of the *anterior cingulate cortex* (ACC), which is located deep inside our foreheads, behind our brains' frontal lobes. Apparently, the ACC has much to do with self-regulation, (the ability to direct attention and behavior, plus tamp down inappropriate, knee-jerk responses). It can also switch tactics in a flexible manner (para. 2).

Those with damage to the ACC show "impulsivity and unchecked aggression," (!) and those with bad connection between this and other parts of the brain don't do well on tests of mental flexibility (they tend to cling to ineffective problem-solving strategies rather than changing their behavior). (para. 2)

Now, meditators, on the other hand, perform much better on tests of self-regulation, resisting distractions and making correct answers more often than non-meditators. In addition, they show more activity in the ACC than non-meditators. Besides self-regulation, the ACC allegedly affects past learning to support better decision-making. Research suggests that the ACC may be particularly important in the face of uncertain and fast-changing conditions (para. 2).

Our focus here in Chapter 5, remember, is mindfulness, and the foregoing offers evidence of the potential benefits thereof.

The Three Major Components of Mindfulness

A major player in the dissemination and science of mindfulness is one Jon Kabat-Zinn. The people at Mindful Leader (2023) provide the following overview:

According to Kabat-Zinn (reported by the Mindful Leaders), mindfulness arises from paying attention purposefully, in the moment, without judgment. In that mode, we are to focus on:

- Intention—choosing to cultivate awareness
- Attention—to the present moment, sensations, and thoughts
- Attitude—being kind, curious, and non-judgmental

Apparently, when these three qualities of mindful behavior intermingle, the way we relate and engage with events is transformed, "creating a more spacious way of being that is gentler and more peaceful" (paras. 1–4).

The Mindful Leaders maintain that each of the three elements described above help us "move out of autopilot and take ownership of our thoughts." Doing this enables us to reflect, observe, and make good decisions, responding *as we wish,* as opposed to "lashing out reactively." Rather, we pay attention to what we're experiencing and choose *peaceful* reactions to things (people, thoughts, events, emotions). (para. 6)

I was struck by the Mindful Leaders' emphasis on *intention*. Part of me thinks, "Well of *course* we have to pay attention (have intention) if we hope to effect change..." but maybe that response is inappropriate. I know from other research that our brains manage by "clumping" experience; in fact, if they don't have a specifically named, neuronal "clump" for something, that something (thought) literally cannot be entertained consciously.

I guess we *can* live on autopilot? I think it more meaningful to look at where we've been, ask ourselves what we think of the miles we've traveled thus far, and see if another road might look more promising. As Robert Frost reminds us, it might "make all the difference" (1916).

Mindfulness-Based Stress Reduction for Recovery

We need to go into a bit more detail now about what actually happens in an MBSR session. Harold (2023) says that any or all of the following may be introduced: breathing techniques; gratitude journaling; group dialogue; home assignments; meditation and/or yoga.

Breathing techniques

In this mode, you could learn "diaphragmatic breathing;" I like the much more colloquial "belly breathing." (Perhaps it reminds me of "belly laughing.") Inhaling causes our bellies to rise and fill with air; exhaling causes our bellies to fall as they deflate. Doing this slows our heartbeats, lowering our blood pressure, and helps us relax. I have this general sense that oxygen is good for us.

Gratitude journaling

We spoke earlier of the value of journaling. I may have used my favorite expression, "How do I know what I think till I see what I say?" The professionals tell us that starting a "gratitude journal" can be helpful. Okay. I'll start right here: I'm grateful for:

- my husband
- my children
- my grandchildren
- my cat
- planet earth
- the Chicago Cubs
- the Philadelphia Eagles
- popcorn
- spare ribs
- lakes, streams, and oceans
- the founding fathers
- Christianity
- television
- WW II Aircraft
- Dr. Carpenter (my MA thesis advisor)
- my Uncle Ed
- the color green

- sunshine
- respectful dialogue

This list could truly be five times this long. I feel better about things already! Harold reminds us that journaling helps us "reframe" our perspectives.

Group dialogue

If you've attended school, you may have experienced the value of class discussions. Just the fact that a group of individuals is communicating, sharing values and experiences, can have great value. *Leading* such discussions, I must add, does not come automatically, and the value of discussions can diminish in the hands of a less-than-accomplished facilitator. In general, however, the thought that "Wow: I'm not the only one who's gone through this stuff!" is a good thing.

Home assignments

Oh no! Homework! Hey, schoolwork does not all occur in the school itself, right? Homework can only help in the therapeutic milieu, so I encourage you to embrace it. As part of your program, you might be asked to listen to guided meditations, watch informational videos, and perhaps complete workbook assignments. And, you'll be all the more immersed in the process of getting better. Use the word "milieu" and people will think you're really smart, or they might think you're pretentious.

Meditation

Your therapy may include mindfulness meditations. In a "body scan meditation," you close your eyes and pay attention to different areas of your body. You're trying to notice any tension and picturing the tension and discomfort leaving your body. You may also be asked to engage in "loving kindness meditations" and make healthful changes to your diet.

Yoga

I am shamefully ignorant about yoga. I do know adherents, however, and they are evangelical about its value. Bushrow (2021) assesses its value as follows. Chloe Hodson Watkins, a yoga instructor and owner of Santosha Yoga in Crozet, Virginia, tells us that we live in a "frenetic and fast-paced world," one which leaves little chance for the digestion and integration of everything we experience on a daily basis. To Ms. Bushrow, it's "almost as if our minds and our bodies create a bottleneck to our experience of life. Yoga and meditation offer us an opportunity to clear the bottleneck" (para. 4).

I love the "bottleneck" metaphor. I think of beavers building those dams and stopping up streams (not all the way, but they do create those ponds). Nature and psychology incline toward free-flowing phenomena.

Practicing Metta Mindfulness

Before we get into the nuts and bolts of metta mindfulness (I should use a more pastoral metaphor than "nuts and bolts"), I should sound a cautionary note about the availability of mental health care in general.

Especially during and after the pandemic, access to mental health practitioners of all stripes has been hard to find. The pandemic is receding as we speak, but the following from Leonhardt (2021) remains relevant to the issue of scarce mental health care.

As reported by Leonhardt, the number of Americans experiencing anxiety and depression is going up, with 42% of U.S. adults reporting symptoms (this is 11% higher than in previous years, according to a recent survey from the U.S. Census Bureau). (para.2)

Apparently nearly 1 in 5 Americans has some type of mental health condition. I don't have world-wide statistics as to numbers of people affected, but with the conflict in Ukraine, international tensions between the U.S. and China, the climate crisis—I can't imagine that our optimism levels have shot up to any degree.

Leonhardt reports that spending on mental health treatment and services was $225 *billion* in 2019, according to an Open Minds Market Intelligence Report. "That number is up 52% since 2009, and it includes spending on things like therapy and prescription medications plus stays in psychiatric or substance abuse rehabilitation facilities" (para. 3).

There are collateral costs to the rising instances of mental health difficulty. "The base statistics don't take into account indirect costs, such as lower workforce participation rates and decreased productivity. Depression alone accounts for some $44 *billion* in losses to workplace productivity," according to a recent report from Tufts Medical Center and One Mind at Work (para. 4).

And care can be costly—even more so than physical health costs. "An hour-long traditional therapy session can range from $65 to $250 for those without insurance," according to therapist directory GoodTherapy.org (para. 5).

Of course, there are resources available and of course, populations will wake up to the severity of this problem. All of us can help in accelerating this awakening by talking more freely about the nature and costs (financial and other) of mental illness. Have you noticed in most families that there tends to be a "fixer"?—one who thrives on locating resources of all kinds, contacting them, and in general lining up needed people and appointments? I have a daughter who can be on her phone in the blink of an eye, speaking to a needed specialist, whether it's a dentist, a chiropractor, a restaurant, a car repair shop, or a faith healer. My eldest daughter is that person in our family.

Taking a Pause

The following is from the people at HelpGuide.org (2023). They remind us that it's a busy world. "We fold the laundry while keeping one eye on the kids and another on the dog. We plan your days listening to the radio and commuting to work, and then plan our weekends." However, in accomplishing these tasks, we may find ourselves closing our connections with present moments—missing out on what we're doing and how we're feeling. "Did you notice whether you felt well-rested this morning or that forsythia is in bloom along your route to work?" (para. 1).

I wanted to include this to remind all of us of the perils of distraction. I know you think I watch too much TV, but there's a commercial running currently that shows a mother with several teenage daughters eating at a buffet-style restaurant. The teenagers are talking on their phones and taking selfies. The only way the mother can return them to the present moment is to remind them that the buffet is serving butterfly shrimp. They shriek "Butterfly shrimp?!" and race back to the buffet.

I'm not advocating a return to the good old days, whatever and whenever those were. But the evidence is increasing that communication technology, including that involvement with social media, is doing all it can to divert us from the here and now to different destinations: propaganda to read, products to buy, connections to make which are not always the most healthful. I know a young man who, emotionally at least, lives and dies based on the numbers of "likes" he gets for certain social media posts.

I spoke earlier about the processing power of our brains. Given the sheer magnificence of that breadth and power, it seems a shame to spend it on what are, in many cases, trifles. The essence of *mindfulness* is to turn us from what can be the insignificant to the importance of the present moment: Who are we with? What are we saying? What do we think about it? Why haven't I noticed the mahogany paneling in this room before?

So the watchword here in Chapter 5 is to be mindful. Pay attention to the tangible realities around you. I'm trying hard to be more appreciative of *people*. Most are doing the best they can with the strength, wisdom, perseverance, and humor allotted to them. I wish this tendency of mine came more easily to me than it does.

We've seen in this chapter that help for mental illness can be scarce and expensive. While this may be the case, help will come with the perseverance and hope of those seeking it. There truly are resources in our communities that too many of us ignore. Scour the offices of city and county government. You are paying for services from these sources with your tax money, which is one more reason to seek them out!

As difficult as finding care might be, it underscores the fact that many who seek and find such care can fail to take full advantage of it, falling back into the maladaptive habits and tendencies that led them to seek it. We'll talk more about relapse in Chapter 6.

6

MANAGING RELAPSE WITH SELF-COMPASSION

STUFF HAPPENS

Do people still read comic books? In addition to Archie and others, I used to read Little Lulu a lot. A main character in Little Lulu was Tubby, a friend of Lulu's who did have something of a weight problem (and yes, I do remember my unfortunate incident described earlier about calling my friend Ronni "Tubby").

In one issue of the comic, Tubby returned from a visit to the doctor in great sorrow, worried sick, you might say. He was upset to learn at the doctor's that he was afflicted with a "feezy." He was in despair, wondering at one point how long he had to live. He moped like this for a time, before learning that he'd misheard the doctor.

The doctor in actuality had told him that "He got *off easy*." I'll wait a minute while you process this. "Feezy," right? "Got *off easy*"? It would be gratifying if you could pick up on these things more quickly.

Tubby had little trouble (in this instance and others) feeling *sorry* for himself. Most of us, in fact, are pretty good at this. My brother, for example. He didn't have the most mellow of dispositions. When an apparently trifling occurrence happened, he was wont to sigh and intone, "It's the little things." The little things in life (broken shoe strings, red lights, bruised bananas, runny noses) could cause him disproportionate distress.

You wouldn't have enjoyed playing golf with my brother. Little during a round of golf, when things were going south, was ever his fault. When a shot would go awry (which was often), it would be the wind, an incorrect yardage marker, a rustling in the woods (perhaps a cougar?), a fairway incorrectly mown, noise from the group in back of us.

For most of us, however, things *do* go awry, and we have a range of potential responses we employ when they do go awry. We don't want to feel sorry for ourselves; we want to treat ourselves with *compassion*.

THE NATURE OF SELF-COMPASSION

The following is from Dr. Kristin Neff (2023). She tells us that having "compassion for oneself is really no different than having compassion for others" (para. 1).

She says that having compassion for others involves our noticing that they are indeed suffering. "When we *ignore* the homeless person on the street, we can't feel compassion for how difficult their life is" (Neff, 2023). Also, compassion involves feeling *moved* by others' suffering so that your heart connects to that suffering (the word "compassion" means to "suffer with").

"Having compassion, we feel warmth, caring, and a desire to help the suffering person (Neff, 2023). Having compassion also means offering understanding and kindness to others when they fail or make mistakes, as opposed to judging them harshly. Last, when you feel compassion for another (rather than pity), you realize that suffering, failure, and imperfection are parts common to all human experience. "There but for fortune go I."

I have to add here that saying "I'll pray for you," while a nice sentiment, may not do a great deal to alleviate another's pain.

Neff concludes that self-compassion means *acting the same way towards yourself when you are having a difficult time, fail, or become aware of something you don't like about yourself.* "Rather than ignore your pain with a "stiff upper lip" mentality, you stop to tell yourself, 'This is really difficult right now; how can I comfort and care for myself in this moment?'" (para. 1).

SELF COMPASSION IN PRACTICE

I am indebted to Catherine Moore (2019) for this next section on concrete steps that can be taken to be kinder and gentler to ourselves. Actually, I think I'm far too kind and gentle to myself already, so I'll dedicate this part entirely to you. You're welcome.

I confess I hadn't really thought about this step before, but Ms. Moore says it may be good to start by asking ourselves how we'd treat *others* who may be in the same or similar boats to our own. We probably wouldn't say, "Snap out of it, stupid!", so we shouldn't say something similar to ourselves. What we do with our friends and associates is *validate* their pain, and also offer help to them to get through the rough patch (para. 9).

We really need to let ourselves make mistakes. Think about that for a moment. If you could calculate how many missteps you take in a day, what would the total be? Let me just posit some possibilities:

- You didn't iron a shirt the night before to wear to work.
- You forgot to take your morning medications.
- You didn't clock in when you got to work.
- You forgot to buy the employee who's retiring a card and a gift card.
- You yelled at your son for not making his lunch before school.
- You didn't notice nor comment on your spouse's haircut.
- You ignore the "service engine soon" warning light in your car.
- You skip breakfast but buy a donut on your way to work, along with sweetened coffee.
- You forget that you were supposed to fast before a late morning doctor's appointment.

These have all happened before the sun has made it one-fourth of its way through its daily route. And here's the thing: No one prosecuted you or berated you, correct? SO DON'T BEAT *YOURSELF* UP! What's the song? "Try a Little Tenderness"? Try that.

Moore says that if a friend gets lazy and fails to call you back, you probably won't instantly assume they're a bad person. You won't be either if you "fall short" somehow. As she phrases it, "Giving yourself permission to be human once in a while is one way to accept your flaws, and remind yourself that you're not alone in being imperfect" (para. 9).

We need to show ourselves empathy and understanding. When others are feeling down, hurt, or upset, we might pat *them* on the back, put an arm around a shoulder, hold their hand (the old HR person here wants to put a warning here about unnecessary human contact). While it will be hard to contort yourself into these kinds of actions for yourself, do them in your mind. Cut yourself appropriate slack. Beware of those familiar narratives you may have used in the past ("I'm such an *idiot!*"); you are instead the luminous child of the universe... Yes, I did just make that up (para. 10).

Have you heard about "releasing statements"? Do you know about affirmations? I have to admit that, iconoclast that I can be, I haven't made consistent use of affirmations. A releasing statement is a third cousin once removed of an affirmation. Should you catch yourself thinking a negative thought such as, "I'm so stupid for being upset about this!", put a different interpretation on it: "It's normal to be upset about this; anyone would be" (para. 11).

What we don't want to do is exaggerate perceived shortcomings, turning them into perceived self-portraits. They are *not* portraits; they are thoughts and behaviors common to everyone, and exaggerating them does no one any good. We need to accept ourselves; of *course* we plan to grow and expand our potential, but where we are right this minute is actually okay (para. 12).

Mindfulness is your friend. Mindfulness practices are a good way to place ourselves—center ourselves—in the moment. These practices include yoga and deep breathing (you just need to remember that they're available!). (para. 13)

Becoming Practiced

The experts think that we can become "practiced" in our responses to perceived failings. I remember our gloomy man in the dandruff commercial: "It's there again; she sees it; I'm turning her off!" Not true! Maybe she loves guys with dandruff! It gives them the rugged, unkempt look favored by sheep herders and sewer workers. At any rate, the experts' advice is to get out of these kinds of ruts. You realize, of course, that your brain *loves* ruts? It much prefers them to having to create a new file folder and begin filling it with new modes of thought. Don't let it fool you; you're in charge (para. 14).

Beware of those sneaky social pressures. We worry about how others are going to perceive us in a moment of distress. HAVE the moment of distress! Do what you need to do! Self-kindness means listening to the beat of our own drummers, as Thoreau reminds us. I don't know why this principle is so hard to adopt. Terry Cole-Whitaker writes about this in her aptly named, *What You Think of Me is None of My Business* (1979).

Ms. Cole-Whitaker speaks of parents following scripts given them by the prevailing culture: "For you to be a good parent, your son must go to college, work in this kind of job, marry, settle down, and live in a house with a white picket fence." ...when the son didn't follow the script, the parents felt they hadn't done a good job, and *they* felt guilty" (p. 20).

Reaching Out

Catherine Moore's final word of advice is, seeming to contradict herself, that we consider reaching out to others. She alleges that this contextualizes our feelings (I love big words like "contextualizes"). Her point is that talking with others helps us realize that there are others on the planet with us. It affirms our sense of connectedness, in her words, "reframing out perceived problems within the 'bigger picture' and building support networks that are invaluable to well-being" (para. 16).

WHAT SELF-COMPASSION ISN'T

In another online post, Dr. Kristin Neff (2023) helps us understand what self-compassion *isn't.*

Self-Compassion Is Not Self-Pity

According to Dr. Neff, the biggest difference between self-compassion and self-pity is that in the latter state, people tend to forget that others can have the same issues that they have. This can lead to them ignoring their ties to others, perhaps assuming that they are the only ones on the planet who are hurting. When we pity ourselves, we bring egocentric feelings to the surface and exaggerate the importance and intensity of our issues. Self-compassion reverses this tendency, emphasizing as it does the related experiences of others, reducing or eliminating feelings of isolation.

Dr. Neff also tells us that, "Self-pitying individuals often become carried away with and wrapped up in their own emotional drama." They cannot step back from their situation and adopt a more balanced or objective perspective. On the other hand, when we see ourselves as "compassionate others," what Dr. Neff calls "mental space" is created to recognize an expanded human context for a person's experience ("Yes it is very difficult what I'm going through right now, but it's normal and natural for human beings to struggle at times. I'm not alone…") (para. 1).

Self-Compassion Is Not Self-Indulgence

Self-compassion is not self-indulgence. Some apparently believe that self-compassion can lead to a "Katy bar the door" mentality, allowing them to engage in any kind of behavior that eases their discomfort. As Dr. Neff phrases it, "I'm stressed out today so to be kind to myself I'll just watch TV all day and eat a quart of icecream."

Downing the quart of ice cream is pure self-*indulgence*, not self-compassion. Self-compassion arrives with the idea that you want to be content over the long haul. We do ourselves little good by indulging ourselves in short-term "solutions" such as taking drugs, drinking alcohol, or simply "vegging out" watching daytime TV. By contrast, thinking of the long haul means that you're not afraid of short-term displeasure, such as that which you feel when trying to quit smoking and/or lose weight.

Different forms of what we could call "self-flagellation" rarely work; apparently we can't shame ourselves into making significantly different life choices: Facing the "hard truths" can lead to more pain than we can handle. Weaknesses can remain sidelined because we unconsciously try to avoid what Dr. Neff calls "self-censure" or self-blame.

Apparently this approach often backfires when we can't face difficult truths about ourselves—we're afraid of hating ourselves if all our perceived "dirty laundry" is allowed to see the light of day. Weaknesses may remain hidden in an unconscious attempt to avoid self-censure. On the other hand, the care central to compassion provides a strong motivating force for growth and change, while giving us the safety we need to see ourselves clearly without fear of self-condemnation (para. 2).

Self-Compassion Is Not Self-Esteem

When you think about this factor, that self-compassion is not self-esteem, it almost becomes self-evident. Self-esteem is all about our opinion of ourselves, about our worth and apparent value—in brief, about how much we like ourselves. Sometimes this can be problematic, in that we appear to be trying to rise above the average; this has to occur should we want to feel better about ourselves.

Dr. Neff says, "This means that attempts to raise self-esteem may result in narcissistic, self-absorbed behavior, or lead us to put others down in order to feel better about ourselves." In addition, we can also come to feel aggression toward those who, in our minds at least, are trying to make us feel worse about ourselves. The "sweep it under the rug" tendency can also come to the fore in order to hide or diminish our perceived shortcomings. A bottom line is that our perceived value (self-esteem) comes to depend far too much on changing circumstances and the impressions of others."

With self-compassion, on the other hand, we remind ourselves that we are all members of the same band: *All* people deserve good will and understanding, not because they are pretty, physically strong, or brilliant. Goodwill and understanding should be available simply because we're all members of the same family. We don't have to feel better than other people in order to feel better about ourselves. Dr. Neff cites research that indicates "that in comparison to self-esteem, self-compassion is associated with greater emotional resilience, more accurate self-concepts, more caring relationship behavior, as well as less narcissism and reactive anger" (para. 3).

SELF COMPASSION AND TRAUMA HEALING

Apparently, recovering from trauma experienced during childhood involves going back to that trauma in later life. This can sound counter-intuitive, for who wants to relive the pain experienced earlier?—Wasn't once enough?

In effect, however, it's a "new you" returning to the time of your life in which you experienced the trauma, in effect looking at it with new eyes. And, I would add, a new heart. This is what experts such as Dr. Arielle Schwartz (2020) ask us to do.

People who have experienced childhood trauma such as sexual and physical abuse can come to blame themselves for what they went through earlier in life, coming to think that they are bad or "dirty," that they somehow brought the abusive behavior on themselves. Thus it can be difficult for them to cultivate a new perception of the individual they were as a child. When you think about it, it seems natural to develop a compassionate, loving appreciation for the one who endured the suffering.

Dr. Schwartz says, "If you were being abused or violated, a reparative experience might involve imagining your 'adult self' rescuing your young self by leaving the dangerous environment... a reparative process involves offering profound acceptance and loving kindness for the hurt feelings held by the young you" (para. 4).

This concept takes more than a moment for us to get our heads around. Those of us suffering in our adult years as a consequence of childhood trauma doubtless have spent considerable time and effort to *escape* what happened to us earlier—and now, in the face of logic and reason, we're supposed to go *back*?

Yes, that's what we're asked to do.

But now we're asked to go back as seemingly whole adults (damaged perhaps, but whole), able to extend a helping hand and a loving heart, so to speak, to our childhood selves. This feels like an extremely positive concept. I picture a waif-like little girl, rag doll in hand, crying in pain, embarrassment, and shame. Who wouldn't be moved by this? Who wouldn't want to sweep her up in their arms and comfort her? Do that for the child you were.

Extending empathy and comfort to your earlier child is a process. You may have been dealing with the trauma of early abuse for a long time, causing it to become deeply embedded in your psyche. Don't set unrealistic expectations for yourself, that you can snap your fingers, re-image the child you were, and move on. Commit to the process, however, and healing will occur.

Overcoming Emotional Flashbacks

Flashbacks are dreams on steroids. Filmmakers have depicted flashbacks in the minds of soldiers who have experienced battle: images, sounds, screams, gunfire that cause the original traumatic experience to live again in soldiers' minds.

Writer Shirley Davis (2021) brings us the following steps to follow should we experience traumatic flashbacks. The steps are the brain children of Dr. Pete Walker.

1. Say to yourself: "I am having a flashback."

With flashbacks we return to a timeless part of the psyche, one that feels as helpless, hopeless, and dangerous as we were in childhood. The hurt happened then; it can't get you now.

2. Remind yourself: "I feel afraid, but I am not in danger!"

Remember, you are safe in the here and now, far away from the danger of the past.

3. Own your right/need to have boundaries.

Remember that you do not have to allow anyone to mistreat you! You can leave dangerous situations and protest unfair behavior. Put them in that rear view mirror.

4. Speak reassuringly to the Inner Child.

That inner child requires that you love her unconditionally, that she can approach you for comfort and protection when she feels alone and frightened.

5. Deconstruct eternity thinking in childhood, when fear and abandonment felt endless—a safer future was unimaginable.

Remember what you've experienced before: Flashbacks always end; you will be returned to comfort and safety.

6. Remind yourself that you are in an adult body with allies, skills, and resources to protect you that you never had as a child.

Feeling small and little is a sure sign of a flashback.

7. Ease back into your body. Fear launches us into "heady" worrying or numbing and "spacing out."

Ask your body to relax and chill out. Experience each of your major muscle groups and encourage them to relax. Breathe deeply; find a safe place to soothe yourself; feel the fear without reacting to it.

8. Resist the Inner Critic's Catastrophizing.

Use thought to stop the inner critic's exaggeration of peril and constant efforts to control the uncontrollable. Refuse to shame, hate, or abandon yourself. Channel the anger of self-attack into saying NO to unfair self-criticism.

9. Use thought substitution to replace negative thinking with a memorized list of your qualities and accomplishments.

Grief is okay. Flashbacks let you release old, unexpressed feelings of fear, hurt, and abandonment and to validate the child's experience of helplessness and hopelessness. Healthy grieving can turn tears into self-compass

ion and anger into self-protection.

10. Cultivate safe relationships and seek support.

Be alone when you need to be, but don't let shame isolate you. Feeling shame doesn't mean you are shameful! Educate those around you about flashbacks and ask them to help you talk and navigate through them.

11. Learn to identify the types of triggers that lead to flashbacks.

Avoid unsafe people, places, and activities that can trigger mental processes.

12. Practice preventive maintenance with these steps when triggering situations are unavoidable.

Remember what you are flashing back to. With flashbacks you have opportunities to discover, validate, and heal wounds from past abuse and abandonment. They also identify still unmet developmental needs and can provide motivation to meet them.

13. Be patient with a slow recovery process.

It takes time in the present to de-adrenalize and considerable time in the future to slowly decrease the intensity, duration, and frequency of flashbacks. True recovery is a gradually progressive process (often two steps forward, one step back).

14. Don't beat yourself up for having a flashback.

Flashbacks happen without your consent and certainly without your desire for them to occur. Don't beat yourself up over something you have little control over (para. 28).

Part of me senses that flashbacks will be difficult to overcome without the guidance of an experienced and caring therapist. If it will be a while before you're able to make that happen, by all means try Dr. Walker's suggestions.

Further content about facing and overcoming trauma has to do with emotional regulation, and we will take a close look at that in Chapter 7.

7

EMOTIONAL REGULATION SKILLS
(BUILD RESILIENCE)

If I were more literate and historically grounded, I'd give an example here of a society that didn't require at least a measure of self-control among those in its population. During the days of the Roman empire, I understand that those toga-clad citizens could party pretty heartily, but they also managed to field disciplined armed forces, govern in sophisticated, structured ways, build imposing temples and arenae (I think that's plural for "arena"), establish impressive irrigation and highway systems, and so on.

In the early days of the United States, the founding fathers worked tirelessly to formulate and then articulate a system that would enable citizens to fairly consistently regulate themselves. They couldn't have a citizenry running amok, breaking rules as fast as they could be formulated. They not only expected the people (gasp), to *select* their leaders and change them out periodically, but they expected people to do so in a sober, reflective manner.

Having said this, I *have* read accounts of what Lincoln's early political life was like. Less than a century after the revolution, American politics was anything but a calm, sedate, consistently deliberative and careful process. There were the unfortunate incidents in the Senate with lawmakers assaulting one another with canes, for example. A duel cost Americans the great statesman Alexander Hamilton, shot by the unreliable Aaron Burr.

Whatever humankind's development and initial creation, we have become these intricately complex creatures, subject to the influence of both emotion and reason. Sadly, we are not adept at incorporating the latter to function harmoniously and wisely with the former. Balance: That's the watchword in using all of our mental, emotional, and physical attributes to inch our ways forward. As we're about to see, it's not so much one quality (emotion) working smoothly with another. Rather, it's far more of a blended approach.

EMOTIONAL REGULATION

In truth, scientific data show that the dichotomy between reason and emotion is something of a fiction. There is not an organ north of the pancreas, for example, labeled Feeling Center, or one named Emotion Gland. Emotion originates in the brain. We even know exactly which parts of the brain affect different emotional responses.

Jill Seladi-Schulman (2018) provides details. Something called the "limbic system" is a group of "interconnected structures located deep within the brain... part of the brain that's responsible for behavioral and emotional response" (para. 4). The system is "... the part of the brain that's responsible for behavioral and emotional responses" (para. 5).

The following parts of the brain are generally considered those that comprise the limbic system (para. 5):

- **Hypothalamus**. In addition to controlling emotional responses, the hypothalamus is also involved in sexual responses, hormone release, and regulating body temperature.
- **Hippocampus**. The hippocampus helps preserve and retrieve memories and affects how

we make sense of the spatial dimensions of our environments.

- **Amygdala**. The amygdala helps coordinate responses to things around you, especially those that trigger emotional responses. It plays a key role in fear and anger.
- **Limbic cortex**. This part contains two structures, the cingulate gyrus and the parahippocampal gyrus. Together, they affect mood, motivation, and judgment.

Have you heard of the Strategic Air Command? SAC (at least at one time), was located deep in the heart of the United States, I suspect due to the fact that it would be safest there from foreign attack (Versus, say, locating it in Washington State or South Florida). The Strategic Air Command was developed to ensure that the U.S., through a robust radar and satellite network, could identify and respond appropriately in the event of a missile or aircraft attack from overseas. In effect, our individual brains can do the same thing.

Parts of our brains work together to both formulate solutions *and at the same time provide us with the emotional wherewithal needed to activate them.*

REMEMBRANCE OF CHAPTERS PAST

I know you remember our discussion of the VW Wolfsburg plant that we had in Chapter Two. I'm not saying that you *must* reread that chapter now, but, honestly, it wouldn't hurt. What we emphasized in Chapter Two was that brain function is not a matter of lock step, predictable sequences of particular stimuli and responses, but actually must be governed by related brain *systems*. The ones introduced in Chapter Two were the Default, Executive, and Salience Systems. The latter was the one I compared to the amazingly complicated control system operative at the VW plant, the one that can produce different vehicle models, of varying sizes and colors, one after another without missing a beat. It produces them, you'll recall, with those zany robots.

I probably should have spent more time defining "salience." This is a term you may have heard in a sentence like, "The salient part of her talk focused on the function of the semicolon." "Salient" means "most important," more specifically, "most important at the moment." Semicolons are vital, incidentally, to your writing career.

The passage below is from Tom Cochrane (2019):

> Reason and emotion are often supposed to be at odds with each other. From one perspective, our emotions are like unruly toddlers, demanding and whimsical, that need to be held in check by the adult intellect. From another perspective, the rational mind is cold and calculating and needs the warmth of the passions to grasp what really matters. (para. 1)
>
> I don't think that either of these perspectives, properly understood, is wrong. Where they are potentially confusing is if they suggest that emotions and reason are two separate sources of agency vying for supremacy. (para. 2)

If I establish no other point than the following, I will be satisfied: We have to abandon the idea that emotion and intellect are separate. This is what Cochrane is saying in the passage immediately above: *We can't assume that reason and emotion, as it were, are these two warring factions fighting for dominance!*

Cochrane continues in this vein, saying, "...humans (and other animals) are single agents and we have not evolved the resources of emotion and reason to fight against each other, but to... protect the things we care about. Given this consideration, I think the correct thing to say is that *reason elaborates emotion*" (para. 5).

"Reason elaborates emotion"! Of course it does! Emotions communicate the nature(s) of things to us (whether they are dangerous, desirable, boring), with our *rational* powers making more definitive distinctions among them. The latter, as Cochrane reminds us, are relative to each of us as individuals. This process "...allows the emotions to massively expand their capacity to track the things the individual cares about, to check whether the initial emotional representation is accurate, to infer consequences, and have further emotions towards those consequences. This, I contend, is the main purpose of reason" (para. 4).

As insightful as I believe the above to be, it only takes us an inch or so along the road to discovering the nature of our emotional lives, including how and why they can spiral wildly in the face of individual stimuli. This section of our study, remember, is to discuss how we can better *regulate* our emotional lives, and, as I hope you've begun to see, we have a great deal of studying to do. Having at least a fingernail grasp of what our overall consciousness is trying to do, and with which tools, and in what sequence is a step along that road.

MANAGING OVERWHELMING EMOTIONS

We're going to descend now from 30,000 feet to around 10,000 in our consideration of regulating our emotions, and discuss some concrete things we can do should we find ourselves affected by them. The advice is offered by Footprints to recovery (2023). Wisely and basically, the Footprinters state, "It is important to have skills to help cope and manage overwhelming emotional responses" (para. 1).

Here are their four basic recommendations:

- Observe and describe the emotions.
- Reframe negative or overwhelming thoughts.
- Become aware of your vulnerability to negative emotions.
- Distract.

Observe and Describe the Emotions

Apparently, an emotional response has multiple dimensions. We need to cultivate the ability to observe and describe them, to better understand that emotions are not static, but tend instead to cycle. If we can not only identify but *explain* to ourselves feelings of tension and warmth when something angers us—or those of clamminess, shakiness, and breathlessness when we feel anxious—we can better deploy needed skills to respond to them. We should be able to counteract unhealthy behavioral responses (e.g., punching someone in the nose) to uncomfortable feelings (para. 2).

Reframe Negative or Overwhelming Thoughts

Here we begin the interplay of thought and emotion described earlier. Once an emotional response is triggered, a number of interpretations of the triggering event occur to us. We need to find the thoughts that are going to remove us from the furor of the emotional moment. For example, should we hear that we have not been chosen for a particular job, it might be easy to cycle into negative, self-defeating thought patterns that *retrigger* hopelessness and worry. Stop it! Instead, begin to retrace the process of how you located this opportunity, the things you did well in the recruiting and interviewing cycle, and what if anything you might do differently next time. Seeing these additional perspectives of the situation will ease your emotional, negative response (para. 3).

Become Aware of Your Vulnerability to Negative Emotions

I love this next idea from the Footprinters. To get a better handle on strong emotion, the common expression is HALT. This acronym stands for: "Are you hungry? Are you angry? Are you lonely? Are you tired?" Asking yourself these questions can ease your feeling of being stressed, plus diminish a tendency to react impulsively. And, by all means, determine if you are under the influence of drugs or alcohol. (Recommendation: Don't be). Aware of our vulnerabilities, we can relax a bit, knowing that it feels worse in this moment than it would if we were rested, sober, or if we had eaten a heavy meal. The idea is to make note of our vulnerabilities and initiate self-care to prevent further emotional distress. HALT: There's your key! (para. 4)

Distract

Distraction is something of a delaying tactic. This is probably an inappropriate comparison, but I think of boxers *clinching*: Especially when momentarily stunned, one boxer is likely to hold onto the other in order (hopefully) to clear their head. The clinch is a better tactic than wildly swinging in hoped-for retaliation, which is likely instead to lead to further punishment from the opponent.

As the Footprinters phrase it, "Distraction can be extremely useful in tolerating the feelings in the moment so we do not act on them in a way that may cause harm to us later." Then they come up with another of those helpful acronyms!

This one is ACCEPTS. Are there <u>activities</u> you can try? Perhaps visiting with a friend, attending a meeting, or treating yourself to a Big Mac or a Whopper? The second letter is C. How about <u>contributing</u> to someone through service work and giving back? Visiting a shut-in? The second C is for <u>Compare.</u> Compare your state with another's perspective: This is the "There but for the grace of God go I" insight.

The next letter from the Footprinters is for E. Try acting opposite to the *emotion* you're feeling. Honestly, to me this feels like a tough one. The basic idea is that if we are feeling sad or low, listening to a song or watching an inspiring film or looking at an uplifting affirmation can help. Honestly, I've never made much headway with affirmations, but that shouldn't deter you from using them if they help.

Our experts also recommend acting opposite to the <u>emotion</u> you're feeling. If you are feeling sad or low, listen to an upbeat or empowering song. You can also try <u>pushing</u> the negative emotions or thoughts away. "This should be a last resort to tolerating negative emotions." You can also try changing your <u>thoughts.</u> Lastly, <u>self-soothing</u> behaviors can help. In the latter context, I think hot baths are preferable to consuming boxes of Twinkies or Cheez-Its (para. 5).

YOUR PAST EXPERIENCES DON'T MAKE YOU WEAK

We've all known people who have suffered intense trauma. Since they have to be out and about for us to have encountered them, our assumption is that a degree of healing has occurred from the pain caused by the traumatic event, whether that was a serious accident, a natural disaster, a wartime experience, a rape, or assault. I think of families who have lived through tornadoes and hurricanes, sometimes suffering serious injuries and major losses of property and opportunities to make a living.

I don't know if I'm impressed or incredulous hearing the reactions of people who've survived severe storms, storms that have flattened their homes and in some cases destroyed their livelihoods. What are their mental and emotional states as they begin the rebuilding process? Does reconstructing a house have a counterpoint in reconstructing one's mental and emotional states? How complete and stable are the "rebuilt" human beings? The wishy-washy answer is, "It varies."

Regardless of whatever else you may have heard, it takes time to recover from events such as those just described. The question I have is, do people emerge changed after traumatic experiences? The simple answer is, "Of course they do!" The next question is, what do the changes look like?

It varies.

Some people can literally be knocked senseless by trauma, suffering intense symptoms of fear and withdrawal for extended periods of time. The affect (outward sign of emotion) can become less exaggerated over time, but evidence suggests that inner healing and adjustment can require years to mature.

I have occasion to visit friends and, in some cases, relatives in retirement homes. I see what to me is a curious wardrobe choice, which tends to be more common among male residents. They often (indoors) wear caps and other apparel displaying the insignia of military units they served in, some during wartime and others during peacetime. Of course there are obvious reasons for doing this, probably the most significant is the fact that they're proud of the service they rendered and want to display physical evidence of that pride.

This phenomenon to me is evidence that trauma can apparently heal, at least that is what the outward, physical evidence suggests. Individuals who have been raped return to their families and occupations. Those seriously injured in accidents often can't wait to be back among their friends, family, and workmates. Joe Frazier survived his defeat in the "Thrilla in Manilla" versus Muhammed Ali, and actually chose to enter the ring again.

My point in this section is to explore the condition of trauma survivors. As we speak, do you believe that they emerge stronger? Weaker? A combination of the two, dependent on season and circumstance?

This is Vanessa van Edwards (n.d.):

Trauma can radically change and re-engineer people's life perspectives, and may even change someone's behavior. Often, adversity causes individuals to re-evaluate their life purpose and mission, becoming less materialistic and more able to live in the present. This is something that cancer survivors often experience. (para. 34)

The answer to whether we emerge from trauma stronger or weaker is that it all depends. It depends on the severity of the trauma we experience and the degree of preparation we may have had to withstand it. It depends on heredity. Our "baggage," positive and negative, accompanies us into each new life experience, including traumatic experience.

In the 1950s, considerable numbers of people in America built bomb shelters in their backyards in anticipation of nuclear attack from the Soviets. That, at least until this moment, appears to have been unnecessary, although the bomb shelters may have proved convenient when Aunt Shirley and Uncle Fred came to visit.

RESILIENCE

Resilience means the ability to bounce back from adversity. While some capacity in this area may be innate, it can also be enhanced by positive life choices we make.

Simply put, the stronger we are both mentally and physically, the better we are able to respond to traumatic experiences. Forgive me for the gruesome example, but I remember the young man who was rock climbing some years ago. After a fall he found himself hopelessly wedged between large boulders, basically unable to move.

In that situation I might have resigned myself to my fate. I was miles from anyone who may have been able to help me. I was basically immobile. In fact, the young man affected, Aron Ralston, *did* give up.

Here is Thompson's account (2022) of Ralston's thought process during this critical moment. Essentially he closed his eyes and waited to die, but then—

...he experienced a vivid out-of-body experience he interpreted as a vision of the future, where he saw himself in a living room with a young son. That inspired Ralston to keep fighting and eventually figure out a way to break his two bones on the rock before cutting through the skin, muscle, tendon, nerves and ligaments to detach his arm. (para. 11)

"I think if you'd told me, 'This is going to happen, Aron,' I think I would have said, 'OK, well, that's a little bit too far,'" Ralston said. "That's again, this beauty of when that crisis, *when that trauma happens*, [my italics] you get to find out and I sit here today, almost 19 years later and I know what I would do if that were to happen." (para. 12)

This is extraordinary, bordering on the unbelievable. The rather pedestrian conclusion I come to though is that Ralston had developed *resilience* to meet the crisis moment, resilience that gave him the strength and courage to move forward.

Hamlet famously tells his friend Horatio in the play that bears his (Hamlet's) name, "The readiness is all." This is not unlike St. Paul advising his adherents to "put on full armament" in the face of their adversary Satan.

Despite courageous and insightful efforts in this direction, many of us arrive unprepared and ill-equipped to meet the challenges we're bound to face. This returns me to what I see as the perils of distraction in modern life. Resilience takes time and directed effort to develop. It takes training. Think of those ancient Greeks... the schooling, the athletic competitions, the military training... the focus.

BUILDING RESILIENCE

The worthies at PsychCentral (2016) offer the following ten suggestions for building resistance (to withstand rock climbing accidents and other unfortunate occurrences):

Make connections. Let me think of an original phrase here... how about "No man is an island"? Help is available in times of crisis! Workmates provide a cadre of support in times of trouble, as do members of civic organizations and churches. This won't happen magically; you'll have to seek people out and engage with them.

Avoid seeing crises as insurmountable problems. Alexis Zorba in the film of that name tells his young protege Basil: "Life *is* trouble! Only death is not. To be alive is to undo your belt and *look* for trouble!" Well, perhaps we don't need to go *looking* for it, but neither should we be surprised when it comes to visit.

Accept that change is a part of living. We used to think that automobile seat belts were too confining. We used to think that pagers were the last word in electronic communication. We used to pick up the phone and say "Hazel, get me 746." I *personally* don't recall doing this, but have it on good authority that others did.

Move toward your goals. I would add a preamble to this suggestion: "*Have* goals!" Life is going by for heaven's sake! Buy yourself one of the Covey organization's planners and fill it up! An astonishing percent of goal accomplishment is related to writing the goals *down*!

Take decisive actions. Learning that you have cancer tends to get your attention. When this happens, turning out the lights and lying for extended periods on your bed may not lead to the palliative solutions that can help. DO SOMETHING! Read the cancer literature; quiz your doctor; evaluate the kind and intensity of therapies that might help.

Look for opportunities for self-discovery. Remember that ill wind that blows someone, somewhere, some good. We learn and grow from any number of experiences, including the ones we classify as traumatic. Many of us are ignorant, and it is our choice to remain so or not. "Ignorance" is simply the absence of information. Find some, especially that which can tell you more clearly who you are and what you can withstand.

Nurture a positive view of yourself. Remember the John Candy character in the film "Trains, Planes and Automobiles" (1987). He says at one point to his disapproving companion (played by Steve Martin), "I like me. My wife likes me." He retains this positivity about himself in the face of any number of difficulties. A model for us.

Keep things in perspective. Whatever happens to me today, it's unlikely to be fatal. I'm grateful for that. I do have difficulty, however, with some topics, such as politics in America. I tend to turn into a raving maniac at the behavior of politicians and the opinions about them communicated by the media. I need to get a grip. Attain reasonable perspective. I feel better now.

Maintain a hopeful outlook. The Psych Centrals want us to stay positive. I need to expect the best from our politicians. I'm going to set to work visualizing productive behavior from them... seeing them approving funds for expanded library collections, paying more attention to the disadvantaged versus that paid to themselves… I know I can do it.

Take care of yourself. We're to attend to our own needs and feelings. Engage in activities we enjoy and find relaxing. Exercise regularly. This will keep our minds and body primed to deal with situations that require resilience. Sign me up.

I'm going to sign *you* up for Chapter 8, which is all about "Evidence-Based Tips and Exercises."

8

EVIDENCE-BASED TIPS AND EXERCISES

REVIEW

As serious and damaging as intense trauma can be (rape, assault, violent weather extremes, life-threatening disease), there are paths forward. People recover from trauma, some emerging stronger from the experience than they were before.

The American Psychological Association (2023) Reminds us of likely effects of traumatizing events:

- intense or unpredictable feelings
- changes to thoughts and behavior patterns
- sensitivity to environmental factors
- strained interpersonal relationships
- stress-related physical symptoms

Trauma can leave us on heightened alert and with accompanying feelings of fear, even terror of the traumatizing event recurring. Among the least of these feelings are increased irritability and moodiness. Knowing that these responses are to be expected is the first step toward facing them, realizing that they are not the traumatizing event itself but reactions that many trauma survivors experience and overcome.

James Baldwin said in one of his novels, "You can't know anything about life and expect to get through it clean." Of course you're going to remember trauma, often vividly. While it seems counter-intuitive, sometimes the memories and their attendant feelings can seem more intense than the disturbing event itself. The memories sometimes come "out of the blue" in the most incongruous of situations, surprising you with symptoms such as increased heart rate and perspiration. Decision-making may be difficult, along with concentration in general. Your eating and sleeping patterns may change. You may overeat or oversleep, or, on the other hand, develop insomnia and loss of appetite.

As for environmental factors, those too can be disruptive. Sirens and loud noises can bring memories of the traumatic event flooding back, increasing latent anxiety. They may also lead to fear that the traumatic event is going to be repeated.

Chances are that you will *appear* relatively unchanged from a traumatic experience, but that can be far from the truth. Family members and coworkers, seeing "the same old you," may expect you to *be* the same person you were before your traumatic experience, and you simply are not. This can lead to your thinking, "Don't they realize what I've been through?" and being upset that indeed they *don't* seem to realize it. This can lead to your becoming more withdrawn, isolated, or detached from your usual work and social routines.

We've all heard the saying "Fake it till you make it," but I think it unwise to practice this in our recovery from trauma. "Making it," becoming a reasonable facsimile of your former self, will require time and understanding, first for yourself, then for friends and loved ones.

You may experience physical symptoms from trauma. These can include headaches, nausea and chest pain, severe enough perhaps to require medical attention. Should you have pre-existing conditions, these can be affected by the stress of trauma.

The APA offers the following four suggestions for response to trauma:

- Lean on your loved ones.
- Face your feelings.
- Prioritize self-care.
- Be patient.

In terms of the APA's first suggestion, not all of your family, friends, coworkers, and fellow students are going to be helpful. Each of us, however, has one or more people in our lives who truly "get us," and these are the ones you should count on for support and understanding. These pilgrims may also volunteer to help you with household tasks or other obligations, which can take some of your daily stress off of you. Let them.

In terms of facing your feelings... difficult but necessary. Of course you don't *want* to face them, but maladaptive behaviors such as staying home-bound, oversleeping, sticking to yourself, eating too many Doritos—these are not going to be helpful, nor is using substances (mind-altering ones, alcoholic ones). Avoidance behavior is to be expected, but understand that it can interfere with and delay your healing. Get support from loved ones; perhaps see a therapist.

You need to make taking care of yourself a priority. I realize that this can venture close to "wallowing," but it need not be if you're careful. Nutrition! Eat those fruits and vegetables! Make sure you get enough sleep! In regard to sleep, you realize of course that it's your evolutionary partner in this very kind of work: Your brain will get to work re-channeling and adjusting networks, but only if you give it time and opportunity.

Get out there into nature! Remember Wordsworth's appreciation of "impulses from vernal woods." Visit lakes, streams, rivers, the beach. I believe the latter have a pull on us because estimates are that men are composed of 60% water and women 55%. When we get near the water our very "natures" rally to our aid! In addition to experiencing these kinds of impulses from vernal woods, go to museums, meditate, take naps.

Last, remember to be patient with yourself. Think how long it can take to recover from broken bones and/or serious diseases, from surgeries. I once thought that I could return to work a week after involved heart bypass surgery. I actually did, but was nervous, wobbly, and nowhere near as effective as I'd hoped to be. Recovering from trauma takes time.

OTHER VOICES

The literature on trauma recovery tends to be remarkably consistent in its recommendations. Resnick (2023), writing for verywellmind.com, lists her suggestions as follows:

- Accept support.
- Find the right help.
- Connect with others.
- Engage in physical movement.
- Work with your feelings.
- Practice self-care.
- Avoid recreational substances.
- Take breaks.
- Practice mindfulness or meditation.
- Engage in creativity.

In terms of Resnick's first point, you don't want to experience support kicking and screaming, or whining that you can handle your recovery on your own. I sense that the issue is that we can look perfectly well following a traumatic event: no crutches, no casts on our arms and legs, no bandages around our foreheads. We know, however, that we're hurting, and that we need at least a bit of help.

Now finding the *right* help is another matter. You are the only one who can make this determination. Aunt Louise might serve perfectly well, or perhaps Grandpa, Grandma, or both. The right help also might include your Labrador Retriever, Luke, who can accompany you on long walks. Or the right help might mean a reputable psychotherapist. There is no shame in seeking out one of the latter. If you don't believe me, find and read Dr. Peck's *The Road Less Traveled.*

Perhaps you were something of a loner before you experienced your traumatic event, but follow up might include a change in this orientation. Is "No man is an island" a saying? A Bible verse? A hit song? A polka? Whatever its source, the idea is a solid one. Even before traumatic events we are social creatures, and following trauma this proclivity should be amplified. You don't have to engage in debates or intensive Q & A with people. Just remember you're part of "the family of man," and that your relatives are there for you.

As for physical movement, I can't recommend it strongly enough. I've learned that creakiness can be insidious, that it can attack when least expected. Go for a walk. Go for a *run*! More years ago than I'll reveal, early in what became a running craze or phenomenon, I decided to don shorts, singlet, and tennis shoes, and go to our local high school's track, run, and see what all the fuss was about. I jogged for four quarter-mile laps, then eight, then twelve, then finally twenty-eight without stopping. Seven miles. Endlessly therapeutic. Endlessly stiff the next day, but still exhilarated by the experience.

Now working with our feelings... What does Resnick mean by this? For one thing, she means *not* running and hiding at the first sign of one, or acknowledging it and then trying to drown it. An interesting thing will happen if you just stop, take a pause and let it (for the moment at least) have its way with you. You will see that it passes, and that it passes fairly quickly. As it recedes in the distance, you'll have added perceptions of where it might have come from and why it had the impact it did on you. It can't do any of that if you block it before it has a chance to express itself.

Self-care we've discussed earlier. It remains curious, however, that many of us find it so difficult to engage in. Maybe it's part of the protestant ethic. Maybe Christianity is to blame ("The Son of Man came not to be served, but to serve"). But in trauma recovery you MUST give yourself high, if not top priority. Take those baths. Read those books (stay away from horror stories).

Take up an instrument! Even if you can't carry a tune, sing something! (Others don't have to be present.)

Travel. You need not go far in your travels; we recall that Thoreau said, "I have traveled much in Concord," and he meant what he said. I think what he meant was, on every occasion he "saw with new eyes," and that's what we do in travel as self-care.

Have I harangued you enough about avoiding "recreational substances"? I would just re-emphasize how quickly they can become habitual, even addicting, perhaps especially when we find ourselves in recovery mode. In this mode, we sometimes tell ourselves that we "deserve a little reward."

Most of us know that even when we start slowly and with small doses, drugs and alcohol have a way of taking over, of taking control. If you've never gone, go to an Alcoholics Anonymous meeting. Even if you don't believe you are an alcoholic, the refreshing candor at the meeting will inspire you. You will also see that you are not the only one on the planet who may be having difficulties.

Resnick's eighth recommendation is that we take breaks in our recovery from trauma. You had a life before your traumatic experience occurred; you have a life other than recovery afterward. What were your recreational pursuits pre-trauma? I would ask about golf, but if your game was/is similar to mine, you may want to take your breaks another way. No need to pile trauma onto trauma.

As I write this, yesterday pro golfer Rory McAlroy, on a par four, 375 yard hole, with his *driver*, struck the ball to within four feet of the hole. I require seven strokes to hit a golf ball 375 yards. Good for Rory. Remember the principle here: Life went on before your traumatic experience, and darned if it isn't still out there doing so.

We spoke fairly extensively earlier about mindfulness and meditation. I suspect the central concept with them is turning our attention to the here and now. What do the phenomena around us look like? Sound like? Feel like? Smell like? What does it feel like when we touch them? Is my cat as heavy as she looks? I would pick her up to see, but she won't let me. Our trauma exists in one place and in one place only, and that is in our heads. Grounding current experience in the tactile, audible, and visible phenomena currently around us displaces the merry-go-round spinning in our heads.

Ah. The last bullet. Engaging in creativity. In graduate school, undergoing all the angst that that can bring, I reached the conclusion on my own that creative activity could be a balm of sorts to my oft-distressed psyche. Unfortunately, I chose the wrong medium. I lugged a log into my apartment and endeavored to become a wood carver. I think I'll spare you the result of that experiment. I was unable to spare my neighbors the sounds of hammer and chisel, of dropping heavy wooden objects onto the floor.

Now, I must say that I had more success later in life with photography! I purchased lighting and turned my apartment living room into a photographic studio! Photography really is therapeutic, especially in light of new technical developments that let you see immediately what you've captured. Your photographs literally show you what your vision is; they give you another way of seeing.

And of course, as a struggling writer (?) I recognize the therapeutic value of putting words on pages. If you've never considered keeping a journal, by all means consider doing so in the aftermath of trauma. No habit is particularly easy to start, but consider seriously starting a journal. It will *ground* you, and this is the overarching thing we're looking for in the aftermath of trauma. The trauma is receding into the past; it isn't real. Your tangible experience *now*, as recorded in words, sentences, paragraphs, and books is real.

All the foregoing can demonstrate that this is true. From Resnick (2022) we learn that "Somatic therapy is rooted in somatic psychology, a body-oriented approach to psychology. Somatic therapies work by addressing the feedback loop that continually runs between the mind and the body."

SOMATIC THERAPY

Glenn Ford was a wonderful actor, specializing a great deal in western movies. He would often play a taciturn sort who appeared to be calm and accepting of most things, but he could be pushed too far. When this occurred (on the part of the bad guys), he would drawl slowly, "Now wait just a doggone minute here..."

Now in regard to something called "somatic therapy," let me say, "Now wait just a doggone minute here..." Haven't I been assuming that traumatic memories reside mainly in our heads, our brains? While I still believe that to be mainly true, Pederson (2021) and others indicate that our *bodies* are also involved! The prefix "soma" refers to all bodily dimensions except those involved in reproduction (we don't know what was in God's nor lexicographers' minds in determining that difference).

You realize, of course, that this is a ground-breaking idea. As Pederson phrases it, "Practitioners of somatic therapy believe that a person's negative emotions—such as those experienced during a traumatic event—can stay locked inside the body" (para. 3).

What somatic therapy proposes to do is help us release the negative emotions thus trapped inside of us. These emotions can animate as neck pain, back pain, or elsewhere, and apparently attacking the physical symptoms helps alleviate the psychological ones. Somatic therapy can involve mind-body techniques that release tension weighing on both our physical and emotional well-being. A therapist might use breathing exercises, meditation, dance, and other forms of physical activity to relieve symptoms.

How Does Somatic Therapy Really Work?

So we have this "intrinsic link" between mind and body... "trauma and other chronic negative emotions can get trapped inside our bodies and affect our mental health even further" (Pederson, para. 6).

Apparently, after a traumatic experience, our nervous systems can become "stuck" in survival mode. We release hormones such as cortisol which in turn ramps up our blood sugar and blood pressure, weakening our immune systems in the process (para. 7).

A real "kicker"? ". . Some of our bad experiences can produce deeply rooted beliefs that our conscious minds can't even access. These might include negative or unhelpful thoughts, like 'I'm a bad person' or 'I'll never be successful'" (para. 8).

Pederson concludes that "...somatic experiencing doesn't usually require a complete retelling of the traumatic event. Rather, the client thinks about traumatic memories that lead to high levels of stress and then learns to diminish the arousal through body awareness and various techniques" (para.11).

A FINAL LOOK AT TRAUMA THERAPY

Since it's late now in our relationship, I want to leave you here in Chapter 8 with a therapeutic model that you should be able to call to mind quickly. Jo Nash (2019) borrows her theory from one Stephanie Nelson (2011), who served as a Behavioral Science Officer in the United States Army.

Nelson arrived at her treatment model from working with veterans suffering from PTSD, which has turned out to work well with both that population and with other trauma survivors. The program comprises four stages for those struggling with PTSD symptoms:

- deal
- feel
- heal
- seal

Here is what is meant by each phase of the model.

Deal—Writing a Trauma Narrative

In this stage, a client writes a narrative of their trauma experience, spelling out key facts about it, including who was there, what happened, where did it happen, and when. The client then lays out thoughts and feelings that they experienced to pull the narrative together.

The narrative is followed by a second written exercise in which the client reflects on how they feel in the present moment, including what they may have learned and how they've grown from the experience as a whole. A therapist should be present throughout this process for support dealing with distressing feelings and sensations that might re-emerge, including flashbacks, anxiety, or panic.

Feel—Imaginal Exposure

Step two includes experiencing the feelings aroused by reading the trauma narrative. "This works by exposing, then desensitizing clients to any uncomfortable, distressing, and frightening feelings associated with the original trauma."

This imaginal exposure means revisiting the experience in the client's mind's eye, using the sensory capacity of the imagination. These exposures to traumatic experiences help clients come to grips with their feelings with the support of a counselor or therapist.

The client reconnects to their *original* emotional responses to the trauma, which otherwise can become displaced onto other triggering stimuli. Often, trauma survivors *avoid* emotional triggers. This can lead to a narrowing of life experience and reduced quality of life. Nelson (2011) clarifies: "To cite one example of how this can work, physical contact with a partner or spouse may trigger a rape survivor, who may then withdraw or "freeze" upon physical contact. This can destroy a survivor's capacity for intimate relationships."

Heal—Channeling PTG (Post-Traumatic Growth)

In this stage, clients reintegrate their feelings and thoughts about the original trauma. This facilitates opportunities for learning and growth. It includes these three stages:

- *Freedom of choice*
- During this phase, a caregiver explains that while the client did not choose their traumatic experience, they can choose how to go forward from it. There is a narrative therapy technique called "rewriting the ending" that can help the client create a new path.

- *Finding meaning*
- Patients are led to find meaning in their experience, in whatever way seems most appropriate.
- *The hero archetype*
- Finally, the therapist guides the client through the journey of the Hero Archetype. The therapist re-tells the client's story in the context of the client's spiritual and cultural values. This is all the more valuable should the hero survive significant trauma and emerge stronger for it.
- "The client may also benefit from hearing stories where the hero experiences a significant trauma and becomes a much stronger person as a result."

After these three techniques have been explored, the therapist can teach the client PTG channeling, redirecting their emotional energy away from avoidance triggers into productive, goal-oriented behavior. This can include client homework exercises to help shift them from survival mode toward post-traumatic growth.

Seal—The Mind as a Filing Cabinet

Finally, Nelson tells us that the post-traumatic growth path includes reorganizing the traumatic memory using the "mind as a filing cabinet" comparison. This compares the memory of the traumatic experience to disorganized information scattered throughout a filing system of the mind. [Author Note: Since you asked, yes, I did come up with this theory on my own years ago now, and have always wondered where it came to rest...]

Rather than the files being neatly ordered in the mind's "office," numerous folders can contain fragments of information that are confusing and disorientating. The "sealing" step reorganizes memories as files and stores them away safely. They can be accessed in the future, but are no longer anything more than one of the *many* files that are stored in the cabinet of the mind.

CONCLUSION

If you have not confronted true horrors, understood evil, suffered hopelessness and despair, found faith, and made yourself completely accountable for your own choices, actions and outcomes, then I can guarantee that any acceptance you pretend to have will be as brittle and temporary as a snowball in the middle of summer.

— GRAEME RODAUGHAN, *THE CRANE WAR*

Let's break the epigraph above into some bullets so we can see it better:

- confront true horrors
- understand evil
- suffer hopelessness and despair
- find faith
- make yourself completely accountable for your own choices, actions, and outcomes

One problem I have with the epigraph is the use of the word "acceptance." Does Rodaughan mean acceptance of ourselves? Satisfaction with how well we've turned out? Or simply acceptance of the fact that to whatever degree we work through the five categories, that will be the measure of satisfaction we experience in life?

Some years ago, a film was made called *An Officer and a Gentleman* (1982). The movie covered the experiences of a number of would-be navy pilots at a training facility in Northwest Washington State. Gere's character, Zack Mayo, is many things we don't want in our military ranks. He has been raised by an itinerant father, moved about considerably in his younger years, and has become in the eyes of his drill instructor, Sgt. Foley, "a good little hustler."

He has difficulty with the training regimen, reverting to "hustles" he's used in prior years to get what he needs from life. His pilot training, and particularly his relationship with his hard-bitten drill instructor Sergeant Foley, finally gives him a different perspective. Rather than kick him out of the unit for a final, egregious transgression, Foley puts Mayo through hours and hours of grueling physical and mental agony, leaving him (Mayo) lying on the ground sobbing with fatigue and a sense of failure.

In a heavy rain, begging Sergeant Foley to give him a second chance, prone in the mud, Mayo moans, "I got nowhere else to go… I got nowhere else to go."

After a pause, Sergeant Foley responds briskly, "Okay, Mayo. Let's get back to the barracks."

Mayo's psychological "stuff" was in large part his own making. Whether *we* contrive our stuff ourselves or have it visited on us from elsewhere (an accident, a catastrophe of nature, a debilitating illness), after all the tactics used to "put us back together again" (see "Humpty Dumpty"), the responsibility for that task (the putting back together) ultimately resides with ourselves.

Close to the end of the film, a tradition for the graduating cadets is to file past their drill instructors, face them, salute, and hand the drill instructor a silver dollar. Mayo does this. After handing Foley the coin, Mayo says, "I never would have made it here without you." Without expression or diverting his gaze, Foley responds, "Get out of here!"

FINDING FAITH

I don't think Rodaughan means "finding faith" in the religious sense. Rather, I believe he means finding faith and trust in the means that have carried us to our current landing place. Those means could well include many of the suggestions we've offered in the different chapters of our book, so we're about to have another quick look at them. Understand that I don't mean to discount at all the role religious faith *can* play in recovery from trauma. I do find it difficult to apply a "one size fits all" approach to trauma recovery.

I'm going to summarize now-salient points from our different body chapters.

INTRODUCTION

I spent much of our Introduction talking about my cat Mira. Let me see if she's still in here...Yes! She's over there on the couch, looking at this text, ready to pounce on the tiniest of punctuation and usage errors. So like her.

I told you about Mira to describe the ways trauma can visit both cats and people in life, and the characteristics both can develop in response. I have to say, Mira showed remarkable resilience surviving the way she did in the alleyway in back of our church. She, of course, has not been able to apply the therapies we've discussed throughout the book, which you of course are free to do.

A friend of ours has two cats who are almost different species than Mira, so dissimilar are they to her in their behavior. You can't take two steps into the friend's house before her cats are greeting you, meowing, purring, asking to be picked up. From birth, they were fed, comforted, supplied with all the necessities of life. Mira had a wildly different row to hoe in her early days and weeks.

1

PTSD VS. C-PTSD

P ost-Traumatic Stress Disorder. Complex Post-Traumatic Stress Disorder. The basic difference between these two responses to trauma is that the former is often caused by one near-cataclysmic event such as an accident or violent storm, whereas the latter grows from repeated trauma over time, such as continuing sexual or physical abuse. In the latter case, irony is present in that the perpetrator of the abuse should occupy a position of love and security in your life, and it is doubly, trebly traumatic that the reverse is dramatically, insidiously true.

Chapter One also indicates that one individual can suffer from each type of post-trauma disorder. After suffering physical and emotional abuse in early childhood, a person can experience a different kind of abuse as an adult, such as surviving an automobile accident or being in battle. While therapies exist to remediate this situation, the individual in recovery can have difficulty making peace with more than one debilitating experience earlier in life.

2

EXAMINING THE IMPACT

The impact of trauma can be varied and intense. I spent considerable time early in Chapter Two establishing how complex our human, intellectual, and emotional processing capabilities are, and how they can be thrown into discombobulation by different kinds and intensities of trauma.

You will recall my description of the VW Wolfsburg plant in Germany. What I find so remarkable about that operation is its ability to carry out multiple and varied tasks to produce a variety of products on the same assembly line. What is needed in the operation is identification of each product vehicle with all its variety: make, size, color, options, and power source (battery versus internal combustion engine). The robots on the production accomplish all their tasks in real time. What that means is that the assembly line doesn't stop; one robot doesn't say, "Can you install this windshield for me?" to another robot; another doesn't reply, "I'd give you a hand but I have these tires to deal with."

No; it all happens in a smoothly coordinated sequence. What the VW engineers have created on that assembly line is a clumsy replica of the human brain's processing capability. I would think the most difficult task for the engineers (computer, system, and manufacturing partners) is coordination, and, in fact, this is what our human brains carry out with every bit as much speed and skill.

Until something happens to them. Those studying our brains identify three kinds of operational systems used in thought and action: These are the default, executive, and salient systems. For our purposes, I indicated that the salient system is perhaps most important, in that it's the one that sees, identifies, and coordinates individual tasks.

The foregoing operating and coordinating forge along as designed, until flies appear in the ointment or sand gets into the gears. In the case of human beings and brain function, flies and sand can appear in the form of "body dysmorphic" disorder and others. In body dysmorphic syndrome, people develop disproportionate angst over the shape, size, and appearance of their bodies, endlessly working to make sure that they look and move the way they should. Cosmetic surgeries can be employed to create (in the minds of those receiving them) ever more desirable features of the face and body.

3

COGNITIVE BEHAVIORAL THERAPY (CBT)

My paternal grandmother wasn't particularly kind (some of the time) to my paternal grandfather. When she would disagree with one of his perceptions or ideas, she would say, partly in fun, partly for dramatic effect, "There's something wrong with your brains!" I know; heartless.

Cognitive behavioral therapy is used with people having "something wrong with their brains." The therapy involves a sequence of Perception > Behavior > Pattern > Confrontation/Remediation. An individual undergoing CBT has had a distortion or a maladaptive response mechanism which leads to (perhaps) an unacceptable act, which can become a pattern, until confrontation and perhaps constructive treatment occur.

In this same chapter I framed the above sequence as leading to a specific *frame of reference* that each of us colors in over time. The different objects, ideas, and people populating our individual frames of reference may require changing out as days and decades pass by, and this can be an outcome of cognitive behavioral therapy.

"Paradigm shift" is another name for accomplishing a major change in something. We went from pagers to cell phones. No seat belts to seat belts. Typewriters to computers. Gas engines to batteries. Shopping malls to the internet. As applied to mental functioning, CBT helps in instances where a no-longer-functioning or inaccurate paradigm needs to be rethought and perhaps replaced.

CBT is the familiar therapy that occurs in a therapist's office. The patient reveals individual thoughts and clusters of thoughts; the therapist says, "Let's take a different look at these..."

4

DIALECTICAL BEHAVIORAL THERAPY (DBT)

I n this chapter, I presented an extremely thoughtful exegesis of psychotherapy writ large. I used two hard-to-understand words and phrases in that sentence. An "exegesis" is simply an explanation of something. "Writ large" means considered in a wider context. Another word critical in understanding each of the foregoing is "dialectical." You'll recall that in Chapter 4, I was at pains to define "dialectical," whose first syllable "dia" means "across," as in "diagram," "diaphragm," and "dialogue." Something "dia" is considered in light of the separate factors *across* a larger whole.

Hence, "dialectical behavioral therapy" or DBT takes into account a variety of elements that comprise the therapy experience. This therapy approach is thus considered *across* the following elements: mindfulness, interpersonal effectiveness, distress tolerance and reaction regulation.

Mindfulness is the degree of awareness we have of what is happening around us. While you might say, "Doesn't everybody have that?", to which I'd reply, "Yes they do, but in sometimes distorted and incomplete fashion." Therapy is meant to bring mindfulness back to more concrete and tactical experience for the patient. Second, those seeking therapy may have difficulty accomplishing what they want to accomplish interpersonally. Third, patients may have only one option to employ in the face of perceived distress, and therapy can teach them new options. Fourth, we all need to develop more than a single note to play in the face of distress. Instead of going from 5 mph to 50 in a matter of seconds, we learn to slow the interval down to something closer to perhaps 25 seconds. And finally, something similar can be developed in our ability to regulate what we actually *do* in stressful situations. Physical violence can be replaced by "What I hear you saying is..."

5

MINDFULNESS-BASED THERAPIES

A primary reason people develop psychological disorders is that they project themselves out of current reality into the realm of the dangerous or near-catastrophic. Mindfulness-based therapies are designed to turn off the projectors, and abide instead in well-lighted rooms or the sunny outdoors.

Are you a meditator? I have had mild success meditating, but enough to know a bit about its value. I once accompanied a friend to a religious service. I hadn't known anything about the theology or methodology of the friend's church. Instead of a sermon, the congregation sat in silence for at least 30 minutes! At first distressed by this, I managed to calm myself and actually appreciate the quiet, amid the symbols and icons in the sanctuary.

On another occasion, I accompanied a friend who had a drinking problem to a group therapy session of fellow alcoholics. A group of perhaps 25 of us gathered and awaited the appearance of the therapist. At length he appeared, tanned, relaxed, wearing a leather shirt with fringe on the sleeves. He scanned the room, shifted a bit in his chair, greeted a couple of the participants, then folded his arms across his chest and just sat there.

I absorbed this for some minutes, then finally blurted out, "Aren't you going to *do* something?! These people have come here for some *help!*" He looked at me mildly and asked, "And you are...?" I told him my name, and then he asked, "What do you think I should do?" What I said then is lost to memory, but it led to a discussion by others of what they were doing there, solutions they'd tried, results they'd achieved, and so on.

With mindfulness (both in practice and in therapy), we try to climb down out of our heads, into our hearts and emotions. We try to acknowledge that our problems may indeed be "all in our heads," and seek other spots for them to hang out, or perhaps for them to leave entirely.

6

MANAGING RELAPSE WITH SELF-COMPASSION

In looking for an overarching theme of Chapter 6, it has to be learning to be kind to ourselves. I'll give you a moment to think about why this is so difficult, and perhaps why it is so important.

Relapse occurs fairly often with those who use and abuse drugs and alcohol. A relative of mine, speaking of a mutual acquaintance of ours during a conversation about financial matters, said of our mutual friend, "She'd be much farther ahead if she hadn't poured money down her throat all those years!" She was speaking, of course, of the expense involved in purchasing different alcoholic beverages. Indeed, the overall return received for drug and alcohol expenditures is hard to visualize. We could classify it as minimal.

Something interesting happens whenever someone speaks at an AA meeting. The individual has to begin, "Hello: My name is Sylvia and I'm an alcoholic." Doing this throws all pretension to the curb. Sylvia is about to speak of additional traits she has in addition to her alcoholism, but that is the first, defining way she establishes herself.

In a similar way, we all, every day, all the time, have to recognize how fallible we are, and we have to be kind to ourselves in light of that fact.

This doesn't mean we make excuses for continuing, maladaptive behaviors. It does mean that self-flagellation in response to those behaviors is not likely to be helpful. Recognition is helpful. Acknowledgment of responsibility is helpful. Perseverance is helpful. Continuing to beat ourselves up? Not so much.

7

EMOTIONAL REGULATION SKILLS (BUILD RESILIENCE)

In Chapter 7, we did a lot to blow up the idea that intellect and emotion are separate, discrete entities, often at odds with one another. The clever phrase I used in the chapter was that they are, instead, "peas in the same psychological pod." We learned that both intellect and emotion reside as close kinfolks in the human brain; that, in fact, they interact continuously and, most of the time, effectively. This led into a discussion of resilience as a trait we should all aspire to.

When you think about it, resiliency truly is a key factor in emotional health. It's a given that we're all going to experience disappointment, heartbreak, perhaps even tragedy during our lives. Bouncing back is always going to be the key to moving forward.

Among other recommendations in Chapter 7, we spoke of the importance of making connections. I think in earlier days and times, this was better understood. In many ways, in modern life, despite the internet and social media, real connection is less easy and harder to arrange. We used to encounter one another face-to-face, which brought with it a requirement to be truthful and authentic (others could "see" when we were being otherwise). We had to learn to negotiate, especially if we were the smaller, less athletic or otherwise less promising members of childhood groups.

To move forward positively in life, we also in Chapter 7 looked at the importance of having goals. You know the saying, "If you don't care where you're going, any road will get you there." My recommendation was that you eschew the once-a-year, New Year's Resolution model, and go instead for those SMART goals and make an earnest effort to achieve them. SMART = Specific, Measurable, Achievable, Realistic, and Timely. I'll wait here; you get started.

8

EVIDENCE-BASED TIPS AND EXERCISES

This summary will be brief. You just *read* Chapter 8! I was surprised to learn of the multitudes of worksheets and other tools available online to assist those recovering from trauma, and I urge you to explore and take advantage of those.

The big takeaway I'd make from Chapter 8 has to do with those "somatic" theories! Our worries are embedded in our skin blemishes and large intestines! That of course is meant to be humorous, but Chapter 8 does elaborate considerably (again) on the intimate relationship and cohesion of all bodily organs and systems. We are, as it were, all of a piece.

So be nice to yourself, will you? Please? If you are so inclined, please write us a review.

A SHORT MESSAGE FROM THE AUTHOR

Hey, are you enjoying the book? I'd love to hear your thoughts!

Many readers do not know how hard reviews are to come by, and how much they help an author.

I would be incredibly grateful if you could take just 60 seconds to write a brief review on Amazon, even if it's just a few sentences!

SCAN BELOW TO CREATE A REVIEW

Thank you for taking the time to share your thoughts!

Your review will genuinely make a difference for me and help gain exposure for my work.

Faye Mack

REFERENCES

American Psychiatric Association. (2023). AMERICAN PSYCHIATRIC ASSOCIATION. *What Are Dissociative Disorders?* psychiatry.org/patients/families/dissociative -disorders/what-are-dissociative-disorders

American Psychological Association. (2023). AMERICAN PSYCHOLOGICAL ASSOCIATION. *How to cope with traumatic stress.* apa.org/topics/trauma/stress

Anwar, Bisma. (2022, April 27) talkspace Mental Health Conditions. *DBT for PTSD & Trauma.* https://www.talk space.com/mental-health/conditions/dbt-for-ptsd/

Better Health Channel (n.d.) Better Health Channel. *Post-traumatic stress disorder.* https://www.betterhealth. vic.gov.au/health/conditionsandtreatments/post-trau matic-stress-disorder-ptsd

Brenner, Ira. (2002, March 1). PSYCHIATRY online. *The Trauma Model: A Solution to the Problem of Comorbidity in Psychiatry.* ps.psycychiatryonline.org/doi/10.1176/appi.ps53.3.3350

Bushrow, Christine. (2021, September 24). James Kirk Bernard Foundation. *Yoga and Mental Health: Why and How It Helps.* https://jameskirkbernardfoundation.org/newsletter/yoga-and-mental-health-why-and-how-it-helps/

Cherry, Kendra. (2022, August 10). verywellmind. *What is Cognitive Behavioral Theory? https://www.verywellmind.com/what-is-cognitive-behavior-therapy-2795747*

Choi, Charles Q. (2013, October 20). NBC News. *The human brain may be more powerful than computer thought.* https://www.nbcnews.com/sciencemain/human-brain-may-be-even-more-powerful-computer-thought-8c11497831

Cochrane, Tom. (2019, February 11). fifteen eighty-four. *What is the relationship between reason and emotion?* https://www.cambridgeblog.org/2019/02/what-is-the-relationship-between-reason-and-emotion/

Cole-Whitaker, Terry. 1979. *What You Think of Me Is None of My Business.* Oak Tree Publications, Inc.

Congleton, Kristina, et. al. (2015, January 8). Harvard Business Review. *Mindfulness Can Literally Change Your Brain* *https://hbr.org/20.15/01/mindfulness-can-literally-change-your-brain*

Covey, Stephen. 2004. *The 7 Habits of Highly Effective People.* Simon & Schuster.

Davis, Shirley. (2021, June 14). CPTSDFOUNDA-TION.ORG. *Co-Occupying Post-Traumatic Stress Disorder and Complex Post Traumatic Stress Disorder.* https://ptsd foundation.org/2021/06/14/co-occurring-post-trau matic-stress-disorder-and-complex-post-traumatic-stress-disorder/

Davis, Shirley. (2022, May 23). CPTSDFOUNDA-TION.ORG. *Dealing with Triggers and Flashbacks.* https://cptsdfoundation.org/2022/05/23/dealing-with-triggers-and-flashbacks/

Davis, Shirley. (2021, January 11). CPTSDFOUNDA-TION.ORG. *Managing Emotional Flashbacks. https://cptsd foundation.org/2021/01/11/managing-emotional-flashbacks/*

DBT Skills Group New Jersey. (2023). DBT SKILLS GROUP NEW JERSEY. *The Four Skills Modules.* https:// dbtskillsgroupnj.com/four-skill-modules/

Dibdin, Emma. (2022, September 7). PsychCentral. *How Does PTSD Lead to Emotional Disregulation?* https://psych central.com/ptsd/affect-disregulation-and-c-ptsd

EMDR Institute. (2020). EMDR Institute. *What is EMDR?* emdr.com/what-is-emdr/

EZ Care Clinic. (2022, January 21). EZ Care Clinic. *Distorted Self-Image: Causes, Symptoms and Treatments.* https://ezcareclinic.io/distorted-self-image-causes-symptoms-and-treatment/

Footprints to Recovery. (2023) Footprints to Recovery. *5 Tips for Coping With Overwhelming Emotions.* https:// footprintstorecovery.com/blog/5-tips-coping-over whelming-emotions/

Frost, Robert. (2004) POETRY FOUNDATION. *Acquainted With the Night.* https://www.poetryfoundation. org/poems/47548/acquainted-with-the-night

GoodTherapy. (2018, June 19). GoodTherapy. *Mindful-ness-Based Interventions.* https://goodtherapy.org.learn-about-therapy-types/mindfulness-based-interven tions&ved

Grande, Dianne. (2022, March 21). CHOOSING *therapy. C-PTSD vs. PTSD: Understanding the Differ-ences.* https://www.choosingtherapy.com/cptsd-vs-ptsd/

Harold, Laura. (2023, January 2). verywellmind. *Health Benefits of Mindfulness-Based Stress Reduction.* https://www.verywellmind.com/benefits-of-mindfulness-based-stress-reduction-88861

Himidian, Eden. (2020, October 29). Wildflower Center for Emotional Health. *Dialectical Behavior Therapy in the Treatment of Trauma.* https://wildflowerllc.com/dialecti cal-behavior-therapy-in-the-treatment-of-trauma/

Johns Hopkins Medicine Health. (n.d.). Johns Hopkins Medicine. *Body Dysmorphic Disorder.* https://www.hopkinsmedicine.org/health/conditions-and-diseases/body-dysmorphic-disorder#

Jovanovich, Tanja, and Norrholm, Seth. (2010, September). ResearchGate. *Tailoring therapeutic strategies for treating posttraumatic stress disorder.* https://www.researchgate.net/publication/46382428_Tailoring_ther apeutic_strategies_for_treating_posttraumat ic_stress_disorder_symptom_clusters

Kennedy, Madeline. (2020, April 28). INSIDER. *The difference between C-PTSD and PSTD and how to treat each condition.* insider.com/guides/health/mental-health/cp-std-vs-ptsd

Lebow, Hilary. (2021, June 21). PsychCentral. *Post-Traumatic Stress Disorder (PTSD).* https://psychcentral.com/ptsd/ptsd-overview#what-is-it

Leonhardt, Megan. (2021, May 10). Women & Wealth. *What you need to know about the cost and accessibility of mental health care in America.* https://www.cnbc.com/2021/05/10/cost-and-accessibility-of-mental-health-care-in-america.html

MINDANTIX BLOG. (2019, May 30). MINDANTIXS BLOG. *The Neuroscience of Creativity.* blog.mindantics.com/tag-

Mindful Leader. (2022, March 1). MINDFUL LEADER. *The Truth About Trauma: Can Mindfulness Help?* [Source for Jon Kabat-Zinn]. https://www.mindfulleader.org/blog/67396-the-truth-about-trauma-can-mindfulness

Mindful Leader. (2023). MINDFUL LEADER. *What are the Three Components of Mindfulness?* https://www.mindfulleader.org/what-are-the-three-components-of-mindfulness

Moore, Catherine. (2019, June 2). Positive Psychology. *How to Practice Self-Compassion: 8 Techniques and Tips.* positivepsychology.com/how-to-practice-self-compassion

Nash, Jo. (2019, November 20). positive psychology. *23 Post Traumatic Growth Worksheets for Therapy.* https://positivepsychology.com/post-traumatic-growth-worksheets/

Neff, Kristin. (2023). SELF-COMPASSION. *Definition of Self-Compassion.* https://self-compassion.org/the-three-elements-of-self-compassion-2/

Neff, Kristin. (2023). SELF-COMPASSION. *Self-Compassion is not self-pity.* self-compassion.org/what-self-compassion-is-not-2/

NIV Student Bible. 2002. Zondervan.

Nowak, Lauren. (2019, January 23). BrightQuest. *Complex PTSD and Dissociation: Understanding Detachment and the Healing Process.* https://www.brightquest.com/blog/complex-ptsd-and-dissociation-understanding-detachment-and-the-healing-process/

Olivine, Ashley. (2022, January 12). GoodTherapy. *What is Mindfulness Therapy?* https://www.verywellhealth.com/mindfulness-therapy-5212796#:

Peck, Scott. 2001. *The Road Less Traveled.* Simon & Schuster.

Pedersen, Tracy. (2022, November 21). PsychCentral. *What is Emotional Dysregulation?* https://psychcentral.com/blog/what-is-affect-or-emotion-dysregulation?utm_source=ReadNext

Posttraumatic Stress Disorder. (2017). Posttraumatic Stress Disorder. *Case Example: Jill, a 32-year-old Afghanistan War Veteran.* First reported in Monson, C.

M. & Shnaider, P. (2014). *Treating PTSD with cognitive-behavioral therapies: Interventions that work.* Washington, DC: American Psychological Association. https://www.apa.org/ptsd-guideline/resources/cognitive-behavioral-therapy-example

Psychology Today. (n.d.) Psychology Today. *Post-Traumatic Stress Disorder.* https://www.psychologytoday.com/us/conditions/post-traumatic-stress-disorder

ptsduk. (2023) ptsduk. *PTSD and C-PTSD: The similarities and the differences.* https://ptsduk.org/ptsd-and-c-ptsd-the similarities-and-the-differences/

Raypole, Crystal, and Marcin, Ashley. (2023, March 10) healthline. *Cognitive Behavioral Therapy: What Is It, and How Does It Work?* https://healthline.com/health-cognitive-behavioral-therapy#concepts

Resnick, Ariane. (2023, February 18). verywellmind. *How to Heal from Trauma.* https://www.verywellmind.com/10-ways-to-heal-from-trauma-5206940

Resnick, Ariane. (2022, October 22). verywellmind. *What is Somatic Therapy?* https://www.verywellmind.com/what-is-somatic-therapy-5190064

Research Gate. (2006, January). ResearchGate. *Post-Traumatic Stress Disorder: Evidence-Based Research for the Third Millennium.* *https://www.researchgate.net/publica*

tion/7445902_Post-Traumatic_Stress_Disorder_Evidence-Based_Research_for_the_Third_Millennium

Reutter, Kirby. (2022, December 8). Psychotherapy Academy. *What Is DBT for Trauma?* https:psychotherapy academy.org/psychotherapy-academy-updates-podcast/dbt-ptsd-ttreatment-for-complex-ptsd

Ross, Colin. 2000. *The Trauma Model.* Manitou, Communications, Inc.

Schwartz, Arielle. (2020, January 5). ARIELLE SCHWARTZ. *Self-Compassion and Childhood Trauma Recovery.* https://drarielleschwartz.com/self-compassion-and-childhood-recovery-dr-arielle-schwartz/%23

Seladi-Schulman. (2018, July 23). Healthline. *What Part of the Brain Controls Emotions?* healthline.-com/health/what-part-of-the-brain-controls-emotions

Singer, Emily. (2013, December 5). Quanta Magazine. *Inside a Brain Circuit, the Will to Press On.* https://www.quantamagazine.org/inside-the-brains-salience-network-the-will-to-press-on-20131205/

Smith, Melinda, et.al. (n.d.). HelpGuide.org. *Post-Traumatic Stress Disorder (PTSD).* https://www.helpguide.org/articles/ptsd-trauma/ptsd-symptoms-self-help-treatment.htm

Society of Clinical Psychology. (July 2017). Post Traumatic Stress Disorder. *What Is Cognitive Behavioral Therapy?* https://www.apa.org/ptsd-guideline/patients-and-families/cognitive-behavioral

Tanasugarn, Annie. (2020, June 5). Psychology Today. *Is it Borderline Personality Disorder or is it Really Complex PTSD?* https://www.psychologytoday.com/us/blog/understanding-ptsd/202006/is-it-borderline-personality-disorder-or-is-it-really-complex-ptsd

Therapy Cincinnati. (2021, October 3). Therapy Cincinnati. *Complex PTSD and Attachment.* https://www.therapycincinnati.com/blog/complex-ptsd-and-attachment

Thoreau, Henry David. 1999. *Walden or, Life in the Woods.* New American Library.

Tufts Medical Center. n.d. Tufts Medical Center. *Post-Traumatic Stress Disorder (PTSD).* hhma.org/healthadvisor/aha-ptsd-bha

Tull, Matthew. (2020, November 23). verywellmind. *Dialectical Behavioral Therapy (DBT) for PSTD.* https://www.verywellmind.com/dbt-for-ptsd-2797652&ved

Van Edwards, Vanessa. (n.d.). SCIENCE of PEOPLE. *Post Traumatic Growth: Move Forward When Bad Things*

Happenn https://www.scienceofpeople.com/post-trau
matic-growth/

Wesley, John. (n.d.). goodreads. *John>Wes-
ley>Quotes>Quotable Quotes.* https://www.goodreads.
com/quotes/12757-do-all-the-good-you-can-by-all-
the-means

www.ingramcontent.com/pod-product-compliance
Lightning Source LLC
Chambersburg PA
CBHW061744120626
46550CB00005B/1888